AF307508

Defoe
Abbott
Marx
Hardy
Machiavelli
Montaigne
Chesterton
Cooper
Emerson
Joyce
Austen
Hugo
Eliot
Grimm
Melville
Haggard
Stoker
Carroll
Christie
Maupassant
Byron
Molière
Wilde
Engels
Schiller
Garnett
Einstein
Fitzgerald
Hawthorne
Smith
Kafka
Goethe
Dostoyevsky
Hall
Cotton
Kipling
Doyle
Willis
Baum
Henry
Nietzsche
Balzac
Leslie
Dumas
Flaubert
Turgenev
Stockton
Vatsyayana
Crane
Burroughs
Verne
Whitman
Gogol
Vinci
Curtis
Tocqueville
Busch
Homer
Widger
Tolstoy
Darwin
Thoreau
Twain
Scott
Plato
Harte
Potter
Freud
Zola
Lawrence
Dickens
Kant
Jowett
Stevenson
Burton
Hesse
Andersen
London
Descartes
Cervantes
Cooke
Poe
Aristotle
Wells
Voltaire
Hale
James
Hastings
Bunner
Shakespeare
Irving
Richter
Chambers
Doré
Dante
Swift
Chekhov
da
Shaw
Wodehouse
Benedict
Alcott
Pushkin
Newton

 tredition®

tredition was established in 2006 by Sandra Latusseck and Soenke Schulz. Based in Hamburg, Germany, tredition offers publishing solutions to authors and publishing houses, combined with world-wide distribution of printed and digital book content. tredition is uniquely positioned to enable authors and publishing houses to create books on their own terms and without conventional manu-facturing risks.

For more information please visit: www.tredition.com

TREDITION CLASSICS

This book is part of the TREDITION CLASSICS series. The creators of this series are united by passion for literature and driven by the intention of making all public domain books available in printed format again - worldwide. Most TREDITION CLASSICS titles have been out of print and off the bookstore shelves for decades. At tredi-tion we believe that a great book never goes out of style and that its value is eternal. Several mostly non-profit literature projects pro-vide content to tredition. To support their good work, tredition donates a portion of the proceeds from each sold copy. As a reader of a TREDITION CLASSICS book, you support our mission to save many of the amazing works of world literature from oblivion. See all available books at www.tredition.com.

Project Gutenberg

The content for this book has been graciously provided by Project Gutenberg. Project Gutenberg is a non-profit organization founded by Michael Hart in 1971 at the University of Illinois. The mission of Project Gutenberg is simple: To encourage the creation and distribu-tion of eBooks. Project Gutenberg is the first and largest collection of public domain eBooks.

Traditions of the North American Indians, Vol. 2

James Athearn Jones

Imprint

This book is part of TREDITION CLASSICS

Author: James Athearn Jones
Cover design: Buchgut, Berlin – Germany

Publisher: tredition GmbH, Hamburg - Germany
ISBN: 978-3-8472-3111-0

www.tredition.com
www.tredition.de

Copyright:
The content of this book is sourced from the public domain.

The intention of the TREDITION CLASSICS series is to make world literature in the public domain available in printed format. Literary enthusiasts and organizations, such as Project Gutenberg, worldwide have scanned and digitally edited the original texts. tredition has subsequently formatted and redesigned the content into a modern reading layout. Therefore, we cannot guarantee the exact reproduction of the original format of a particular historic edition. Please also note that no modifications have been made to the spelling, therefore it may differ from the orthography used today.

Designed & Etched by W. H. Brooks, A. R. E. A.
She is gone! that beautiful form is but shadow. *page 87.*

CONTENTS
OF
THE SECOND VOLUME.

TALES OF AN INDIAN CAMP.

LEGENDS OF THE CREATION.

I. THE TWO CHAPPEWEES.

A TRADITION OF THE TRIBE OF THE DOG-RIBS.

Upon a narrow strait, between two tempestuous and stormy seas, lived the young man Chappewee, whose father, the old man Chappewee, was the first of men. The old man Chappewee, the first of men, when he first landed on the earth, near where the present Dog-ribs have their hunting-grounds, found the world a beautiful world, well stocked with food, and abounding with pleasant things. There is nothing in the world now which was not in it then, save red clay, a canoe with twelve paddles, and the white man's rum. Then, as now, whales were disporting in the liquid element; musk-oxen filled the glades, and deer, and bears, and wolves, were browzing on the hills, or prowling about the forest. But there was at that time no canoe, for there was nobody to paddle it; no rum, for who would drink it? and red clay was not found till a long time afterwards, when the young man Chappewee's nose bled, and coloured the earth, a portion of which has since been red.

When the old man Chappewee came upon the earth, he found no man, woman, or child, upon it. Knowing that it was not good to be alone, he created children. To these children he gave two kinds of fruit, the black and the white, but forbade them to eat the black. Having issued his commands for the government and guidance of his family, and laid up plenty of provisions for them, he took leave of them for a time, to go into a far country where the sun dwelt, for the purpose of conducting him to the world, which was yet unvisit-ed by his beams. So, taking with him three thousand large roasted porpoises, oceans of black fish, thirty large whales, and a good deal of tobacco, that he might do by the way those necessary things, eat and smoke, he departed for the residence of the sun. After a very long journey and a long absence, he returned, bringing with him the glorious orb, which ever since has lighted the earth, in some countries, for a portion of the hours of each day, and, in other countries, for a part of the days of each year. When he returned, he found to his great joy that his children had remained obedient; had eaten only of the white fruit; and were therefore, as yet, beyond the reach of disease and death. So he left them again, to go on another distant expedition. He saw that the great luminary he had given the world lighted it only for a part of the hours of each day; and, in the frozen regions of the North, only for a portion of the days of each year. Now, in the land from which the old man Chappewee fetched the sun, he saw another orb, formed to be the lamp of the dark hours. It was to conduct this second sun to the borders of his land, that he again bade adieu to his children and dwelling, and departed upon the second expedition.

While the old man Chappewee was absent on his first expedition, his children ate up all the white fruit, and he forgot, before he left them on the second, to replenish their stock. For a long time they resisted the imperious calls of hunger, but, at length, their cravings for food became so importunate, that they devoured the forbidden gift — the black fruit. Chappewee soon returned, bringing with him the beautiful bright round moon, the lamp of the dark hours, and the glory of the season when the sun is away. He had no sooner come, than he saw in the eyes of his children that they had transgressed his commands, and had eaten the fruit of disease and death. He saw it in the countenance of one stretched out on the bed of sickness; there was speedy death written in the eyes of another; and the slighter pains incidental to the human frame on the brow of a third. He was very much displeased with them, and told them, that in future the earth should produce bad fruits; that sickness should lay them on beds of leaves, and pains rack their bones; that their lives should be lives of fatigue and danger, and their deaths, deaths of doubt and agony — penalties which have attached to his descendants to this day.

Having brought the sun and moon to the earth, the old man Chappewee rested from his labours, and made no more distant expeditions. Many, very many, years he lived, and death came not to him. But, to all around him, the consequences were what he denounced, and he had the unhappiness to see his prediction verified. The earth produced bad fruits; the cranberry and the whortleberry rotted on the frost-nipped bushes, and the strawberry shrivelled on the mildewed vine. He saw trees grow up crooked, that, before the disobedience of his children, grew only straight; and animals, which before were only sleek and round, now were poor and emaciated. He saw sickness lay his children on beds of leaves, and pains rack their bones; he saw their lives, lives of fatigue and danger; and their deaths, deaths of doubt and agony. He saw their spirits again in the mist of the Falls, and heard the music of their voices, while their bodies lay in the sacred shed. Still death came not to him. He had now lived so long, that his throat was worn out, and he could no longer enjoy life, but he was unable to die. His teeth had rotted out, and had been renewed a hundred times; his tongue had been re-peatedly chafed out, and replaced; and of eyes, blue, white, and grey, he had had very many pair. Finding that life was a gift which he could not part with easily, perhaps, not without some stratagem, he called to him one of his people—it was not his son, nor his son's son; no, nor one of the twentieth generation—all these had passed away.

"Go," said he, "to the river of the Bear Lake, and fetch me a man of the Little Wise People. [1] Let it be one with a brown ring round the end of the tail, and a white spot on the tip of the nose. Let him be just two seasons old, upon the first day of the coming Frog-Moon, and see that his belly be not too big, and see that his teeth be sharp. And make haste, that I may die."

The man did as he was directed. He went to the river of Bear Lake, and brought a man of the Wise Four-Legged People. He had a brown ring round the end of his tail, and a white spot on the tip of his nose. He was just two seasons old, upon the first day of the Frog-Moon, and his teeth were very sharp, as any one would find that put his fingers between them. He brought him by force, for he was very unwilling to come to the old man Chappewee, who gave the following directions for his treatment.

"Take the Wise Four-Legged Man," said he, "to the head of the Coppermine river, and dip his four paws in the bubbling spring which gives it birth. Give him a little neshcaminnick to drink, and comb his hair, and scratch his belly, to put him in good temper. Whisper in his ear words of encouragement. Tell him not to disgrace himself, nor shame the heroism of his race by cries, nor tears, nor groans, but bear pain like a man. And, when you have spoken the words of comfort, pull from his jaws seven of his teeth."

So they did as the old man Chappewee bade them. They went to the Beaver, and spoke to him thus:

"Wise Little Man of the Four-Legged Race, the old man Chappewee has commanded us to dip your four paws in the bubbling spring, which gives rise to the Coppermine, to give you to drink a little cup of the pleasant juice of the neshcaminnick, and to put you in good temper by combing your hair and scratching your belly. And he begs that you will not disgrace yourself, nor shame the boasted sagacity of your race, by cries, nor tears, nor groans; but bear pain like a man, as you are. And we are directed, after our words of peace have been spoken, to pull out seven of your teeth."

To this speech the beaver replied, as every other man in captivity replies. He professed himself "much pleased to part with seven of his teeth to oblige the old man Chappewee, and had no objection to dip his paws in the head waters of the Coppermine, provided he were carried thither. A draught of neshcaminnick none but a fool would refuse; and the having his head combed, and his belly scratched, was almost as good as a feast." Which was all mere stuff, as every body knows.

The things which Chappewee asked being all performed, they brought the seven sharp teeth of the Wise Four-Legged Man to the old man Chappewee. He bade them call all his descendants around him; and, when they were gathered together, he thus addressed them: —

"I am old — the old man Chappewee indeed. My throat is worn out, and I can no longer enjoy life; my tongue has repeatedly been chafed out, and renewed; my teeth have been replaced a hundred times; and I have looked upon the beautiful things of the earth, and the glorious ones of the sky, upon trees, and flowers, and fruits, and the bright stars, and the pale moon, and the glorious orb of day, with eyes of many different colours. But I am tired of life, and wish to sleep the sleep of death. When I look upon the beings and things around me, and see the pain, and sickness, and sorrow, and want, which have become the bitter portion of all, since the disobedience of my children, I lose the wish for a new pair of eyes, nor ask longer use of the fading vision of those which are now in their sockets. I will go hence. Take the seven teeth of the Wise Little Four-Legged Man, and drive them—one into each temple, and one into the middle of my forehead, one into each breast, one into the hollow of my back, and one into the great toe of my right foot." They did as he bade them, and drove the teeth into his body at the appointed places. The old man gave three groans when the tooth was driven into his great toe, and then he died.

Upon a narrow strait, between two noisy and tempestuous seas, lived the young man Chappewee, whose ancestor was the old man Chappewee, and with him resided his family. He lived by hunting and fishing, but more by the latter, because of the great ease with which he caught the various kinds of fishes, which travelled from one sea to the other, through the narrow strait. He had but to cast his net into the water, and to draw it out full; his spear, thrown at random into the strait, might almost be said to be sure of attaching to it a good fat fish. Once upon a time, having constructed a weir to catch fish, such a vast quantity were caught, that the strait was choked up, and the water rose and overflowed the whole face of the earth. To save himself and his family from the dreadful deluge, he embarked them all in his great canoe, taking with him all manner of beasts and birds. The water covered the earth for many moons, and their food was nearly exhausted, a few roasted sharks, and a little boiled sea-ooze, being all that was left them. Still there was no sign of the abating of the victorious element from the face of the conquered earth. No land was visible, and the sun, which sometimes by his beams upon the waves indicates where land lies sunk beneath the ocean, gave not now the evidence of subsiding waters. The young man Chappewee, finding how matters were going, said to his family, "We cannot live thus, we must find land again, or we shall die; we and all the animals we have with us." So he called a great council of all the creatures, and proposed that one of them should dive into the great abyss, and fetch up some mud to make a world of. The ox, being asked to undertake the hazardous service, declined, because, he said, his tail was in the way; the mammoth refused because of his trunk; the elk and deer pleaded their horns; the legs of the musk-ox, were 'too short'; in fact, all the animals made some excuse except the beaver. He professed his willingness to encounter a risk, which must be encountered by some one, and, without any ado, down he went, amidst the applauses of all the animals. Soon his carcase was seen floating on the surface of the waters, and they knew that he had fallen a victim to his courage and intrepidity.

Another attempt was necessary, and, after much persuasion, the musk-rat was induced to make it. He was gone a long, very long time, and was supposed by them to have met the same fate as the unfortunate beaver; but, just as they had given him over, and were preparing to chuse by lot a third animal for the same errand, he appeared, nearly dead with fatigue, but he had a little earth in his paws. The sight of the earth very much rejoiced the young man Chappewee; but his first care was about the safety of his faithful servant, the rat, which he rubbed gently with his hands, and cherished in his bosom until it revived. He next took up the earth, and, moulding it with his fingers into a ball, he placed it on the waters, where it increased by degrees, until it formed a little island in the ocean. His next care was to furnish this island with man, beast, and bird. A wolf, which he was anxious to put out of the way, he being a sad snarler, was the first animal which the young man Chappewee placed on the infant earth; but the weight of the creature was so great, that it began to sink upon one side, and was in danger of turning over. To prevent this accident, the wolf was directed to keep moving with a quick step round the island, which he did for a whole year; and, in that time, the earth increased so much in size, that all on board the canoe were able to disembark upon it. After a long and perilous drifting of the canoe hither and thither, its voyagers were at length able to lay their heads down at night upon solid land, and to sleep unrocked by the tempestuous billow.

Chappewee, on landing, saw that there were no trees on the earth: he would have some. He stuck a piece of a stick into the ground; it became a fir-tree, and grew with such amazing rapidity, that its top soon reached the skies. Once upon a time, Chappewee being out hunting, saw a squirrel, and gave chase to it. The nimble animal ran up the fir-tree, pursued by the hunter, who endeavoured to knock it down, but he could not overtake it. He continued the chase, however, until he reached the country of the stars. As he went, he saw many curious things, meteors, comets, departed friends dancing their dances in the Northern sky; clouds of every kind and colour; spirits flying about the air. Now he felt keen winds, and now warm breezes; now he passed a company of storms marching down upon the earth; or a lightning or two straggling back again to the skies; or a thunder riding a cloud; or a troop of hail rushing to battle with a deal of bluster and fury; or a crowd of snows looking for colder weather and a roosting-place. At last, he reached the country of the stars. He found a land far more beautiful than that he had left behind him, upon the narrow strait, between the two tempestuous and stormy seas. He found it one vast plain, over which led a wide and smooth-beaten road, but he did not see the squirrel. After feasting his eyes awhile upon the surrounding splendours, and regaling his ears with soft music, which came he knew not whence, nor from whom, he bethought him of setting, in the road, with a view to catch the squirrel, a snare made of his sister's hair. This done, he descended the tree till he came to the earth. The next morning the sun appeared as usual in the heavens; but, at noon, it was caught by the snare which Chappewee had set for the squirrel, and the sky was instantly darkened. This, never having happened before, created much surprise and consternation among the people that dwelt at the narrow strait, between the two tempestuous and stormy seas. Chappewee's wife said to him, "You must have done something very wrong when you were up the tree, for we no longer enjoy the light of the day. The glorious orb, which the old man Chappewee brought to us, before his children ate of the black fruit, has disappeared. Alas, for us, who have lost our best friend, the sun! Alas, for us, who, it may be, are involved in a night that will never know an end!"

The young man Chappewee replied to his wife, "I have indeed done something very wrong, but it was not intentionally. I see through the whole business. The sun is caught in the snare I set for the squirrel. It must be liberated, and enabled again to light our steps, for a certain number of the months of the year, and a portion of the hours of each day."

With a view to repair the fault he had committed, he called to him the carcajou, and bade him go up the tree, and release the sun by cutting the snare.

The courageous cat of the mountains readily obeyed, but the heat of that luminary was so intense, that it reduced him to ashes. After him the bear, the wolverine, the wolf, and the panther, were severally sent, but they all experienced the same fate. The efforts of the more active animals being thus frustrated, Chappewee knew not what to do, nor could any one in the great council tell him. After a long period of silence, the ground-mole got up, and said he would make the attempt. Whereupon, there was a loud and general titter among all the beasts, that such an awkward and grovelling creature as he was should propose to himself such a dangerous and distant task. The wolf laughed in the shape of a hideous growl; the fox chuckled as much as if he had committed a successful theft; the horse neighed and kicked, as usual with him in moments of extravagant joy or anger; and the bear shook his sides till they nearly split.

"Week, week, week, what a fool!" squeaked the pig.

"Bah, what a nincompoop!" cried the sheep.

"Bow, wow, wow, where's my tail?" cried the dog, running round to find it, as he always does when much delighted. All the animals, in some way or other, testified their scorn of the good little creature who had kindly made the offer. But, awkward and grovelling as he was, and much as they laughed at him, he succeeded in performing it, by burrowing under the road in the sky, until he reached and cut asunder the snare which bound the sun. He lost his eyes, however, the instant he thrust his head into the light, and his nose and teeth have ever since been brown, as if burnt. During these transactions, Chappewee's island had continued growing, till it had increased to the present size of the great island.

And now the young man Chappewee prepared his island for the residence of creatures. He first traced out the courses of the rivers, by drawing his fingers through the earth, and scraped out the lakes with his spoon. When he came to the mountains, he made a stop. "What shall I do with these heaps of earth?" demanded he of himself. After reflecting a long time upon the labour which would attend their removal, he concluded to let them remain. Hitherto, all the animals, beasts, fishes, &c. had dwelt indifferently on the land or in the water. The shark and the porpoise, though very clumsy and easily tired, could nevertheless walk some, and the whale, though his waddling gait would have made you laugh, yet contrived to go over a considerable piece of dry ground in a short time. Chappewee now allotted to the quadrupeds, birds, and fishes, their proper stations and habitations, and, endowing them with certain capacities, he told them that they were in future to provide for their own safety, because man would destroy them whenever he found their tracks; but, to console them, he said to them kindly, "when you die, you shall be as a seed of grass, which, when thrown into water, springs again into life." The animals objected to this arrangement, and the hog who did the talking said, "No, let us when we die be as a stone, which, when thrown into a lake, disappears for ever from the sight of man." So it was ordered that the ceasing of the beast to breathe should be his utter annihilation, and that the dog only should be the companion of man after death.

The family of the young man Chappewee complained of the penalty of death, entailed upon them by the old man Chappewee for eating the black fruit, and they petitioned for an alteration of the sentence; on which he granted, that such of them as dreamed certain dreams should be men of medicine, capable of curing certain diseases and of prolonging life. In order to preserve this virtue, they were directed not to tell their dreams until a certain period had elapsed. To acquire the power of foretelling events, to gain the eye which should see the dark secrets of futurity, to hear the words of fate in the cry of the winds, and to see the character of unknown things in the aspect of the heavens, they were ordered to insert a live ant under the skin of the left hand, without letting any one know that they had done so. And, whenever they felt it stirring in the flesh, they were commanded to bind over their eyes the skin of a young badger, lay down their heads upon a bundle of the leaves of the black hornbeam, and sleep as soon as possible. The first dream which they should have thereafter would always prove true.

For a long time, Chappewee's descendants were united as one family, but at length, some young men being killed in a game, a quarrel ensued, and a general dispersion of mankind took place. Some—a great many—went beyond the mountains, which the young man Chappewee neglected to level. Others went to the brink of the ocean, where the walrusses dwelt; others again to the lands which have the beams of the sun from the Buck-Moon till it comes again. Some went to the shores of the sea that is never thawed; and some to the brink of the waters that never freeze. One Indian fixed his residence on the borders of the Great Bear Lake, taking with him only a dog big with young. In due time, this dog brought forth eight pups. Whenever the Indian went out to fish, he tied up the pups, to prevent the straying of the litter. Several times, as he approached his tent, he heard noises proceeding from it, which sounded like the talking, the laughing, the crying, the wail, and the merriment of children; but, on entering it, he only perceived the pups tied up as usual. His curiosity being excited by the noises he had heard, he determined to watch and learn whence those sounds proceeded, and what they were. One day he pretended to go out to fish, but, instead of doing so, he concealed himself in a convenient place. In a short time he again heard voices, and, rushing suddenly into the tent, beheld some beautiful children sporting and laughing, with the dog-skins lying by their side. He threw the dog-skins into the fire, and the children, retaining their proper forms, grew up, and were the ancestors of the Dog-rib nation.

II. SAKECHAK, THE HUNTER.

There was, in the land of the Caddos, a good and devout hunter and fisherman, named Sakechak, or "he that tricks the otter." He dwelt with his family upon the little hill Wecheganawaw, on the border of the lake Caddoque. He was a tall man, spare in flesh, but very active, and able to endure more fatigue than the wolf or the wild cat—able to live six days without food, and feast the next six days without intermission. None had eyes like Sakechak to follow the trail of a light-footed animal over the frozen earth; none like him could strike, unerringly, a salmon at twice the depth of a man. Nor was this hunter without the qualities of a warrior. When the Padou-cas came, with hostile intent, to the borders of the lake Caddoque; among those who first took down the spear, and braided the scalp-lock, was Sakechak, the hunter of the little hill Wecheganawaw. He it was who first sounded the war-whoop; he it was who took the first Padouca scalp; he it was who pursued farthest the retreating enemy, and he who returned from the weary pursuit to dance longest the dance of Triumph. And Sakechak was as wise as brave, and as good as wise. Never was he caught suffering his feelings to escape from his controul or management; his word was esteemed in the council as the word of wisdom; his warning of danger was regarded as the cry of the owl. Never did he mock the wretched, or laugh, or scoff at the insane; he was always respectful to the aged; and he daily cried to the Master of Life, from the high grounds, with clay spread thick upon his hair, and at every successful hunt offered, to the same Great Judge and protecting guide of man, the best part of the animals he had caught. That Great Being regarded him with more love than he regards other mortals, and showed it by many signs. The fish he speared were always fatter than those taken by other hunters; the deer that lay at the foot of the wife of Sakechak could not be lifted like other men's by a mere boy. The thunder that shattered, and the wind that prostrated, the forest-trees in other places were never known to do the like by the tall oaks that sheltered the hill Wecheganawaw. The corn of this good hunter came out of the ground two suns sooner than other men's, and the tobacco in his garden was ripe, yellow, and fit for use, while that of his neighbours was green, and food for the worm. The Caddoques, and the other Indians, might have seen enough of the rewards bestowed upon goodness, in the person of Sakechak, to have made them leave off their wickedness. But no, they kept on sinning, until the Great Being deemed them unfit longer to live upon the earth which he had created for their use.

Once upon a time, as Sakechak was about to rest his limbs for the period of darkness, he felt the stirring of the ant which lay under the skin of his left hand, and, binding over his eyes the hide of the young badger, he laid his head upon a bundle of the leaves of the black hornbeam, and slept as soon as possible [2]. His dream was strange and wonderful, and it was accomplished. He saw the Master of Life, being the first Caddoque who had ever seen him. He was a very tall and big man, shaped like an Indian in all save his hands, which were each a sharp spear of terrible proportions, and his tongue was an immense arrow. His eyes were bright as the sun, and each much larger; his hair was very long, and swept the earth, and he wore a great white hat [3]. Each of his feet was larger than the lake Caddoque. He spoke to the dreamer in his lowest whisper, which, nevertheless, was louder than the loudest thunder, and his words were these: —

"Sakechak!"

The hunter replied, "I hear."

"The world is getting very wicked, Sakechak."

"I know it," answered the hunter.

"I hear no longer the voices of men supplicating me for favours — soliciting my lightnings to cool the air, nor my rains to refresh the earth, nor my suns to ripen the harvest. They no longer thank me for the fat bears, and mooses, and deer, and bisons, which I send to their hunting-grounds, nor the salmon, and other juicy fish, which I bid to their waters, nor the corn which I command to grow tall and sweet for their use, nor the rich grapes which I make to bow their vines to the earth. I must sweep, and wash, and purify, the earth; I must destroy all living creatures from off the face of it."

Then Sakechak said, "What have I done, Master of Life! that I should be involved in this general destruction? Have I not offered thee the best of my spoils? — Have I ever neglected to solicit thy favour upon my labours, or to thank thee for the rich gifts thou hast showered upon me and my family — health, plenty, and cheerful hearts?"

The Master answered, "No, Sakechak, thou hast indeed been a good servant; it hath never been my purpose to destroy thee; I will except thee from the general doom: but I will thee to assist in the destruction of thy brethren. Listen!

"Go now, and cut thee a young hemlock, from the spot which my lightnings struck in the last Fever-Moon. Let it be not more than ten seasons old — straight, well-grown, a finely-proportioned trunk, with thriving branches, full of cones, and with leaves of dark green. Knock off the cones, and bring them, together with the trunk and leaves, to the bottom of the hill Wecheganawaw, when the sun of the morning is tinging the eastern clouds with his brightness. Burn them in a fire made of the dry branches of the oak, kindled with the straw of the wild rice. When the heap is completely reduced to ashes, take the ashes, and strew them in a circle around the hill Wecheganawaw. Nothing need be gathered within the circle of the hill, for the living creatures will, of themselves, retreat to it for safety; and, when this is done, take the trunk of the hemlock, divested of its branches, and strike it into the earth, at the spot where the large tuft of green grass is seen growing on the dry and barren hill. There lies the great fountain of the waters; and when the staff is struck into the earth, the fountain shall burst forth, and the earth be swept, and washed, and purified, by the great deluge that shall overwhelm it. Sakechak and his family shall alone, of all the inhabitants of the earth, be saved, and the creatures he assembles around him on the little hill Wecheganawaw be alone those exempted from the all-sweeping destruction."

So saying, the Great Being retreated from the vision of the sleeping hunter, who awoke with the dream fixed on his mind, and, in obedience to the orders he had received, prepared to do his part towards its accomplishment. He went to the spot which the Master had pointed out—the place which the lightnings had stricken in the last Fever-Moon—and he cut from the grove of hemlocks a young tree, full of cones, with a finely shaped trunk, and with thriving branches and dark green leaves. This trunk, with the leaves, he brought to the hill Wecheganawaw, when the sun of the morning was tinging the eastern clouds with his brightness. He burnt them all, save the trunk, in a fire made of the dry branches of the oak, kindled with the straw of the wild rice. When the heap was completely reduced to ashes, he took the ashes and strewed them in a circle around the hill Wecheganawaw.—Then he took the staff, or trunk of the hemlock divested of its branches, and struck it deep into the earth, at the spot on the hill where the large tuft of green grass sprung up amidst barrenness. When he did so, the great fountain was broken up, and the waters burst out in a mighty volume. Slowly and gradually the element began to cover the earth, while the hunter and his family looked on. Now the low grounds appeared but as they appear in the season of showers, here a little water, and there a little water; soon they became one vast sheet. Now a little hill sunk from view, then the tops of the trees disappeared; again a tall hill was observed to be hiding its summits in the overmastering water. At length the waves rose so high that

Sakechak could see nothing more: he stood as it were in a well. The waters were piled up on every side of him, restrained from harming him, or his, by the magic belt of hemlock ashes. While the waters had been rising, the animals in the vicinity of the hill had been running to it for shelter; and there now stood gathered around him a pair of each of the different species of animals.

"Sakechak!" said a voice, which the hunter knew to be that of him he had heard in his sleep.

The hunter answered, "I hear."

"When the Moon is exactly over thy head, Sakechak, she will draw the waters on to the hill Wecheganawaw. She is angry with me because I flogged a comet to whom she had taken a liking, and wishes to be revenged on me. I cannot prevent that unless I destroy her, which I cannot do, for she is my wife, and bore me many sons, which are the stars thou seest, and she is besides necessary to the existence of the world, which shall re-appear swept, and washed, and purified, for the use of thee and thy descendants. Sakechak!"

The hunter answered, "I hear."

"Bid every living creature which is on the hill take off the nail from the little finger of his right hand, if a man; if a bird, or beast, of the right foot or claw. When each has done this, bid him blow in the hollow of the nail with the right eye shut, pronouncing these words — '*Shake Tebe skahpeshim ose,*' that is, 'Nail become a canoe, and save me from the wrath of the moon.' The nail so besought will become a large canoe, and in this canoe will its owner be safe."

The Master of Life ceased speaking, and the hunter rose to see that his commands were obeyed, both by his family and the beasts. Soon was each supplied with a vehicle of safety, by the side of which he stood as the influence of the mother of the stars caused the waters to flow in upon the hill Wecheganawaw. The canoes rose buoyant upon the element, and soon floated upon the surface of the waters which covered the face of the earth. That they might not be dispersed Sakechak caused them all to be bound together by thongs of buffalo-skin.

They continued floating for a long time upon the surface of the waters, till at last Sakechak said, "This will not do — we must have land. Go," said he, to a raven which sat in her canoe near him, "and fetch me a little earth from the bottom of the abyss. I will send a woman, because the eyes of a woman are so curious, and searching, and inquisitive, that if it is wished to find anything hidden in utter darkness, and lost to all else, a woman will be sure to find it before you have counted your fingers over twice."

The raven, proud of the praise bestowed on her sex, answered, that she had no objection to undertake the commission. So, leaving her tail-feathers at home, she dived into the abyss. She was gone a long time, but, notwithstanding her being a woman, she returned baffled of her object. Whereupon Sakechak said to the otter, "My little man, I will send you to the bottom, and see if your industry and perseverance will enable you to accomplish what has been left undone by the wit and cunning of the raven." So the otter departed upon his dangerous expedition.

He accomplished its object. When he again appeared on the earth, he held in his paw a lump of black mud, as large as the tip of the thumb of a full-grown man. This he gave into the hands of Sakechak. But the hunter of the hill Wecheganawaw was without the wisdom which would make the mud avail to the re-production of the world. He fell on his knees, and besought the Great Master of all to endow him with the knowledge which should lead to the re-establishment of things as they were before the deluge. The Master answered not; but his intentions to communicate his wishes to the good hunter were made known by the ant. So Sakechak slept and dreamed, and this was his dream:—

He saw again the Great Master, who bade him divide the lump of mud into five portions. The central portion—that which came out of the middle of the lump—he was commanded to take into the hollow of his hand, to wet with spittle, and to mould into a cake, a little highest in the middle, and flattened all around the edges. He was commanded, when he had done this, to blow a bubble upon the water, and set the little cake afloat in the bubble; with these words:—*I-yah ask-ke*—"I make an earth." He was not to suffer the little world to break away, but was to attach it to his canoe by a string formed of the sinews of the mud-turtle. As it increased in size, he was to strew upon it the remaining portions of mud, which he was enjoined to be very careful to crumble fine, and rub thoroughly to dust. The voice told him, that in less than three moons the lump would be so swelled that he might disembark upon it, he and all the creatures that were with him.

Sakechak did as the voice of the Master bade him. He divided the lump into five portions, and that which came out of the middle of the lump he moulded into a cake, a little highest in the middle, and flattened all around the edges. He blew the bubble upon the water, and he set the cake afloat in the bubble, having first fastened it to his canoe with a string formed of the sinews of the mud-turtle. As it increased in size, he strewed upon it a part of the remaining portions of the lump, first crumbling them very fine, and rubbing them thoroughly into dust. The wind, which was high at the time, blew the yellow dust, which was lightest, into his eyes, and thence the eyes of the Indian have always been tinged with yellow. The little cake increased rapidly in size. One day, as Sakechak had taken up the third portion of the mud to prepare it, by crumbling and rubbing, for strewing upon the earth, his wife discovered a star — the first which had been seen since the breaking up of the fountain. The loud shout of joy which burst from her, and her cry "A star! a star!" so discomposed Sakechak, that he forget what he was about, and threw down the lumps, unrubbed or uncrumbled. This carelessness occasioned the unevenness of the earth; the mountains and the rocks which are now found upon it are the lumps which he threw down unrubbed. He, however, strewed upon it the remaining portion, which is the reason why rocks are found so far below the surface. And the earth, so formed from the mud brought up by the otter, grew so fast that, upon the seventh sun of the third moon, the hunter Sakechak, and his family, and all the beasts, birds, and other living things which were with him, left their canoes for the dry and stable earth, which thenceforth became, and has since continued, their residence.

Upon the earth thus created trees soon sprung up; but they were only trunks destitute of branches. But the wit of Sakechak soon gave them what they wanted. He shot arrows into the trunks, and these became branches, and took the nature of the trunks. Each became an oak, or a pine, or a tulip, or a sweet gum, following the nature of the trunks. Many seasons passed away, however, before the hills were all clothed with trees, or the dense cloud of leaves hid the bosom of the valleys.

The earth was re-peopled from the loins of Sakechak; from him, from one family of Caddos, are all men descended. No matter whither they have been carried; whether they have covered their tent with leaves beneath the warm sky of the south, or built it of ice, where the earth never thaws; whether they are red like myself, or white like the wise man at whose bidding we are gathered together; they are descended from one man, the hunter Sakechak, of the hill Wecheganawaw.

III. THE BIRD OF AGES.

The waters were spread over the face of the earth; there was nothing to be seen but one vast and entire ocean, save the mighty Bird of Ages, which had lived from the beginning of time, whose eyes were fire, whose glances were lightning, and the clapping of whose wings was thunder. He had lived long in the skies above the stars; but, when he heard the rushing and dashing about of the waters, he descended from his seat to the ocean, and touching it, the earth instantly rose, and remained on the surface of the water. It rose of its present size, covered with verdure, as the low grounds which have been flooded by winter rains are green when these rains are withdrawn from them. The mountains, then as now, towered to the skies, and the valleys were deep, and the rivers rushed impetuously over the steeps which attempted to impede their course. Winters locked up a portion of the earth, and the summer suns beamed fiercely and intensely upon another portion. The stars shone by day, and the beams of the moon gladdened the hours of darkness. Winds swept the vast expanse of ocean, and a part of the time was calm as a part of the time is now. The world was very like what it is at this day, save that, within its mighty boundaries, over all its far limits, neither on mountain, hill, valley, tree, nor bush, in den nor burrow, in water nor air, dwelt a living creature. No gentle song of bird arose to break the stillness of morning, no cry of wild beast to disturb the unbroken hush of midnight; the noise of the winds chasing each other over the vast waste was all that was heard breaking the monotonous repose of the earth.

"This will not do," said the bird, talking to himself; "here is a fine world and nobody to occupy it. Here are stars, beautiful as anything can be; a moon, that sheds her mild light on—what?—and a sun so bright that not even the Bird of Ages can look steadily on his beams—with that bird alone to behold him or them. How balmy is the air which I feel fanning my feathers!—but it cannot breathe to revive the human heart after sickness or toil, or gladden the spirit of the beast which lies panting in the shade from excessive heat. It is lost, wasted, and so are the beams of the sun, the moon, and the stars; and so are the sweet fruits that grow spontaneously about the earth, and the beautiful flowers that waste their fragrance on the desert air. This must not be," repeated the Bird.

So he flew up to the highest pinnacle of the Mountain of the Thunders, and there fell to musing, the while scratching the side of his head with his mighty claw. At last he bethought himself of a spell or charm, which was taught him by his father, who lived before time was, and survived its commencement many ages. He recollected that this venerable and wise bird, who did not die till his claws were rotted off, and his feathers all dispersed to the winds, told him that if one of his descendants were to eat nothing for seven days, and to quench his thirst with the dew which should lie upon the mountain-laurel, he would enjoy the power to accomplish that which ought to be done. "Nothing can be clearer," said the Bird of Ages to himself, "than that the world ought to be inhabited. Now I, by fasting seven days, and quenching my thirst with the dew of the mountain-laurel alone, shall, according to the word of my father, be enabled to see this earth tenanted by beautiful creatures; the seeds, which now lie dormant in the earth, will spring up to furnish food for innumerable creatures, and those innumerable creatures will enjoy the bounties spread out in such profusion before them! How delightful it will be to see and hear the birds of soft notes and splendid plumage, singing and hopping about on bush and tree; and the kid, and the fawn, and the lamb, gambolling on the sunny hill-side, and the fishes disporting in their own element; and Man, the lord of all, painted on his cheek and brow with the ochre of wrath, and wearing the gallant scalp-lock, decked with the plumes of the eagle; and to hear his cry of battle, rising from the gathering place of warriors, and to mark the pole of red scalps, and better yet the resolution of the captive, when the torments are inflicted upon him, when the pincers tear his flesh, when the hot stones sear his eye-balls. All these pleasures will delight the eyes and ears of those who shall live on this beautiful world, when I shall have done what I conceive ought to have been done."

So he commenced his fast. Seven days he ate no food, and quenched his thirst with only the dew which lay upon the mountain-laurel. Upon the morning of the eighth day he began his task. "There ought to be a vast number of fishes," said he, "and of different sizes, for each must feed upon the other and smaller." So he called into existence all the fishes that people the waters. Then he said to the quadrupeds and four-footed beasts, to worms and snakes, and every thing else which are not fishes, "Be, for you ought to be;" and they were. So the earth became peopled and inhabited. All were called into existence then, and in that manner, except the Chepewyans, and they had their origin ages after, from the loins of a dog; which was performed thus:

There was among the Crees a man, whose upper lip was split, displaying the upper teeth to every one that saw him; he was not a courageous man, but feared every thing in the shape of danger; even the cry of beasts and the singing of birds, and the growl of the bear, and the song of the bittern, alarmed him. He was very fond of dogs, and possessed the power of transforming them into the shape of men, though he was without the power to make them continue in that shape for a longer period than that between sun and sun. He could make a wolf-dog step into the form of a handsome hunter; he could clothe an old cur with the skin of a very wise *powwow*. After his charm was spoken over a spaniel sneaking with his tail between his legs, you would see, in his stead, a white man doing the very same mean act of cowardice, with his back upon his enemy. A hoity-toity little she-puppy would become in a twinkling a very pretty girl; and an ugly old snarling she-wolf, a crabbed and sour old squaw. But, when the sun arose, the handsome hunter became again the wolf-dog; and the very wise powwow, the old cur; and the white man running from his enemy, the spaniel sneaking off with his tail between his legs; and the very pretty girl, the hoity-toity little she-puppy; and the crabbed and sour old squaw, the ugly and snarling old she wolf-dog. He would have been very glad to have made them retain the form of human beings, but he possessed not the power. At last, he bethought himself of the mighty Bird of Ages, who dwelt among the lofty peaks of the Mountain of Thunders. To this bird he repaired, and telling him what he had come for, he received the command to go to the Lake of the Woods, and bring thence a flat, white stone, which lay upon the southern shore of that lake. It possessed, the mighty Bird said, the power to enable almost any thing to be done which should be asked of it by men of the Cree nation; by the great ancestor of which it had been endued with its present power.

The man did as he was bidden. He went to the southern shore of the Lake of the Woods, and brought away the great white *memahoppa*, or medicine-stone, which has ever since remained with the Crees. Having placed this stone in the corner of his cabin, and addressed it as his tutelar deity, he proceeded to make the transformation of a fine, handsome, courageous, young dog into the shape of a man. When this was effected, he led the man to the memahoppa, and first praying the sacred stone to protect him against the power of change, he placed the man upon it. The charm was effective. The wonderful properties of the medicine-stone operated to keep the man a man. And this man married a woman of the Crees, and from them are the Chepewyans descended.

When the mighty Bird of Ages had finished his work of calling into existence the different creatures, he made a great arrow to be the sign of the deeds he had done; with the command that it should remain lodged in the great council-house of the Chepewyans, until time should be no more. As long as they should obey this command, they should ever be victorious over their enemies, and fortunate in all their hunting expeditions; their word should be law to all the tribes and nations, from the Frozen Sea to the land of the Shawanos, from the towns of the Iroquois to the Mountains of Thunder. But, whenever they should by carelessness lose it, they should be doomed to encounter their full share of the losses and defeats, and difficulties, and disappointments, which belong to other and less favoured tribes. They should sometimes be overcome by a force of inferior numbers; and often seek the beasts of the chace for many weary days without finding them. And, saying thus, he gave the arrow into the hands of the chief man of the Chepewyans.

For many, very many ages, the Chepewyans scrupulously remembered the injunctions of the mighty Bird respecting the arrow, and kept it treasured up in the house of the great council. While they did so, they were the most fortunate tribe on the earth, and became lords over all, conquerors in every battle, and the most fortunate hunters the world has ever known. But, at length carelessness got the better of prudence, and they suffered the arrow to be stolen; the sacrilege so enraged the Bird of Ages, that he quitted the earth, and winged his way to the place he inhabited before he descended from above. He has never been seen on earth since; but the Chepewyans, and other tribes whom this tale has reached, believe that the thunder of the hot moons is the clapping of his wings, and the lightning which accompanies it, the glancing of his eye. When a dark cloud that has no rain crosses the earth, they say he is flying between it and the sun; and they believe that the snow of the winter is the down which he strips from his breast.

IV. THE GREAT HARE.

Michabou, or the Great Hare, sat upon the face of the waters — he, and his creatures, which were all four-legged. The form of this Being was unlike that of any thing ever seen on the earth, before or since. He had four legs, or rather two legs and two arms, but he used them all as if they were legs, and he used the two arms for purposes for which legs could not be used to advantage. So he had four legs and two arms, and yet there were but four in all. Each of his creatures was unlike the others: all were known and distinguished by something which did not belong to another. Some had but one leg, some had twenty; some had no legs, but many arms; and some had neither legs nor arms. The same diversity prevailed with regard to the eyes, and mouth, and nose, and ears. Indeed they were a strange crowd of creatures, and not the least strange of all was Michabou himself, the head chief, or rather great father of all the creatures which moved over the face of the mighty waters.

Michabou was married to a woman quite as odd and deformed as himself, who bore him many children, of strange and various shapes. When the time had come for her to bring forth her one thousandth child, she had a strange dream. She dreamed that the child within her refused to see the light, till he had something firm and stable to stand upon—something which would permit him to enjoy rest undisturbed by motion. She told this dream to her husband, whom it puzzled very much. At length he made out that he was to create a world. He knew before, that the bottom of the ocean was covered with sand. So he dived down, and brought up from thence a glittering grain to serve as the germ of the world.

Having taken this grain of glittering sand into the hollow of his hand, Michabou blew upon it until it so expanded, that it became a little earth. He then set it afloat upon the waters, where it continued increasing in magnitude, until it was large enough to sustain, without sinking, the child which the wife of the great chief, after bearing about her for forty seasons, brought forth to the light of day. This child, upon being born, had the form of a man, and was placed upon the earth thus created. He was the first being which had ever borne the form of a man, and the first occupier of the earth. They gave him the name of Atoacan, which signifies the "great father, or beginner of a race." When he was born, he was larger in stature than any man that has been born since, and he increased in size, until his head towered above the tallest woods.

But Atoacan was alone, and life soon became a burthen to him. He was solitary and sad, and found no pleasure in the beautiful things which were daily, hourly, springing up on the earth. He saw the flowers bloom, and scent the air, but they afforded no pleasure to his eyes, no refreshment to his soul. Sweet fruits were bending the bushes to the earth, or clustering on the boughs, but they were tasteless; for it was in his nature to enjoy nothing, prize nothing, unless participated in by another—the counterpart of himself. So he put clay upon his head, and cried loud to his father, the Great Hare, for a companion. Michabou, perceiving that he and his strange-shaped creatures would be supplanted in power by the son whom he had begotten, the new creature *man*, had ascended to the heavens: he heard the prayer of his son, and listened to it.

There was among the people of the skies a beautiful maiden, whose name was Atahensic. She was fairest of all the daughters of the air, beautiful as the sun, mild as the moon, and sportive as the stars. Michabou asked her if she would descend to the earth, and become the companion and wife of his son; and she, delighted as women always are, at the prospect of a journey, no matter whither, consented. So Michabou made a long string of the sinews and tendons of the various land animals, and by this string he lowered Atahensic into the arms of his delighted son.

The man, no longer solitary, but furnished with the being, intended by the constitution of nature and the Great Master of all for the companion and comfort of his life, set about appropriating to his use the various things he saw. He was no longer solitary, but met the difficulties which spring up in the path of human life, and the labours which he is compelled to bestow upon the procuring of food, with cheerfulness and alacrity. He now went in the morning to the forest glade to hunt the red deer, and his toils were not thought of, because, when they were ended, when the woods, made dark by the coming shades of night, rang shrill with the lay of the fire-bird, and his shafts were all spent, he could bear home the spoils they had won, and be rejoiced by the smiles of his companion and wife.

Atahensic bore her husband two children, a son and a daughter. These two married, and built themselves a lodge far from their parents. They had many children, but Michabou, who came down now and then, to see how things were going on, observing the slow rate at which the world was peopling, determined to adopt another plan. So he told Atoacan that, upon the death of every animal, he must skin it. He must burn the skin, drop a drop of his own blood upon the carcase, and cover it up carefully with dry leaves from the forest trees. Upon the fourth day after he had covered it with leaves, if he would remove the leaves, he would find beneath them a sleeping infant, which, upon waking, would utter a cry of surprise, at finding itself no longer a beast but a human being. Each of these beings would possess the power to assist in the like multiplication of the species, but be denied other power of procreation. Having thus left directions for the speedy peopling of the world, Michabou again ascended to the heavens, which he has not left since.

Atoacan and his son carefully obeyed the commands which had been laid upon them, and of every beast or four-footed creature that died he formed a human being. These human beings were gifted with the qualities and passions which belonged to them in life: these they have retained, and thence it is that, at this day, the dispositions of men are so various. We see one crafty and subtle—he has the blood of the fox; another cruel, malicious, blood-thirsty—he is descended from the wolf. The red skin is courageous—the horse was his father; the white man is a coward—his mother was a sheep. One is full of sprightliness and agility—he is of the blood of the mountain-cat; another is clumsy—the musk-ox was his father. Strange and various are the dispositions which men have—cunning, subtle, sly, wise, brave, prudent, careless, cowardly, peaceable, blood-thirsty. These are qualities derived from the beasts, which died as beasts, and became men and the ancestors of the tribes living on the earth.

V. THE SIX NANTICOKES.

Once upon a time, there was a very bright and sunny day on the earth, and, upon this day so bright and sunny, a strange thing happened. It was in the country inhabited by the tribe of Nanticokes, and upon the borders of the Great Lake. It was in the morning of the day, and the moon was the moon in which the shad, leaving the waters which are salt, make their journey to those which are fresh. Beautiful was the day; the salt and bitter waters lay as motionless as a little child sleeping on the bosom of its mother. The winds were hushed in the caverns of the earth, and the beams of the sun fell gladdening and refreshing every thing beneath them. They shone upon field and forest, hill and valley; upon bird and beast, and fish and reptile, and many other things, beautiful or ugly, curious or strange; but they fell not upon man, for he was not. The tall and erect form, which commands obedience from all other creatures, was not then seen walking among the glades of the forest, with the firm step and haughty eye which distinguishes him. Beasts were many, birds were many, fishes were many, but of men, the lords of all, there were none.

Before the sun descended behind the mountains of the West, he shone upon man also. Six Indians, the first men that were ever on earth, and the ancestors of the tribe of Nanticokes, all at once, they knew not how, nor by what means, found themselves sitting upon the same shore, upon the verge of the ocean. Whether they were created on the spot, or came from some other place beyond the seas;

whether they had swum up from the waters, or crawled out of the mud, or bounded from the depths of the forest, or alighted from the regions of the air, and were changed into men, receiving a gift to forget their former state, they knew not, or if they dropped from the skies, and forgot whence they came through dizziness and the violence of the fall. But this they knew, that they found themselves sitting on the shores of the Great Lake, in the country now inhabited by the Nanticokes, on the latter part of a warm and pleasant day, in the moon in which the shad leave the waters which are salt, and make their journey to those which are fresh. And they knew that there were six of them, and this was all they knew.

These six Indians were all men; there was not amongst them, nor on the earth, a single woman. The song-sparrow, and the mocking-bird, and the dove, and the crested wren, and the spotted lynx, and the gorgeous woodpecker, and the fish with shining scales, and all the other beautiful creatures that have since lived, and now live, were then upon the earth, even in greater numbers, and possessed of greater beauty than now; but woman, more beautiful than any, the most glorious thing that walks the earth, lived not then. It was soon that these Indians found out their wants, and began to provide themselves with food and clothing by means of hunting. They built themselves canoes, and made them bows and arrows, wherewith they took the spoils of land and water; and they set springes for birds, and traps for those creatures which live alike on the land and water. And they cultivated the various plants which they found growing spontaneously—corn, and tobacco, and roots; and gathered ripe grapes, and abundance of delicious berries. They lived well enough, and had they been wise would have sought no further; but they took it into their heads, that they could not live without women. So, led by the gloomy and solitary feeling of a vacant heart, they left the cabins which they had built, and wandered forth in search of the coveted objects. That their chance of success might be greater, they agreed to separate, and each to travel on different paths, and so they parted. One went towards the clime of the snows, another towards the land of the summer winds, the third sought the distant east, the fourth bent his steps towards the mountains of the setting sun, the fifth descended into the bowels of the earth, and the sixth climbed a sunbeam. Before they separated, they agreed that those who were living when the Moon of Grapes again came round, should repair to the same great tree in the shade of which they were then sitting, and there, while the pipe of friendship was passing around, recount their adventures.

The Moon of Grapes again came round, and found, upon one of its pleasantest days, these six Nanticokes sitting beneath the great tree, on the bank of the river which gives its name to the tribe. With them sate six beautiful women, and laughing, and sporting, and rolling about on the green and grassy sod at their feet, lay six beautiful children. The six Indians and their wives appeared very happy, and while they passed the pipe about, laughed and talked very loud and joyfully, and were very, very merry, as though they had been drinking something much stronger than water. At last, one of them, whose name was Sinipuxent, rose and said:

Brothers! it was in the Moon of Grapes of the last year, that we found ourselves sitting on the shore of the Great Lake, endued with the faculties that we now exercise. It was in the Moon of Grapes, that we departed in quest of the beloved beings who are now the light of our eyes. And we agreed, that those who were living when the next Grape-Moon came round should repair to the same great tree, beneath whose shade we then sate, and there, while the pipe of friendship was passing round, we should relate what had befallen us. The Great Spirit has permitted our return to that spot, and the beautiful beings, whom we have brought with us from countries so far apart, are proofs that adventures have befallen us, which are worth recounting. Brothers, you shall hear of what befel Sinipuxent, who left you to climb the sunbeam.

When he parted from his five brothers, he climbed a sunbeam for many days, until he came to the land where the glorious luminary of the earth, the Sun, takes his refreshment of sleep and rest during the dark hours. It was in the morning of the day, and the great light of the world had risen from his couch, and set out upon his journey, but his wife and his children were all, save one, stretched out in profound sleep. That one, the most beautiful of all creatures—look at her, and say if she is not!—sat bathing her lovely cheeks and stately neck in the morning dew, and brushing off the stray drops with the white lily of the lake. Her little feet were carelessly thrust into the clear stream gliding by her, beneath which they glittered like the sparkling sands washed from the mountains into the river of the Nanticokes. Her long bright hair, coloured by the beams of her father, the Sun, lay floating over her naked shoulders and bosom, more beautiful—but ye behold her. Beautiful creature! she saw not the Nanticoke till he stood at her side. When she raised her head, and found a stranger standing near her, she would have fled, but he detained her gently with these words:

"Beautiful creature! what is it thou fearest? I am not he that would harm thee. On the contrary, I would encounter any risk, brave any peril, rather than harm one of the glossy hairs that is straying over thy beautiful brow. My heart tells me, gentle creature, that thou art the object for which my soul hath panted, ever since I first knew that I was. I love thee, deeply and fervently, and wish thee to be mine. I ask thee to leave the clime of thy father, and go with me to the pleasant land and beautiful river of the Nanticokes. Though its skies be not so bright as those in which thou wert born, yet are they mellower. And the waters of the land are clear, cool, and sweet, and the shades are refreshing. The vines are bending to the earth with rich ripe grapes, berries are loading every bush, and the earth is covered with flowers. Thou shalt become my companion in the cabin I have built me beside the Nanticoke; and even as that river, when unvexed by the swell of rains, glides along in the months of summer, so shall our lives pass away. Thou shalt be the wife of my bosom, and together will we live, till we are called to the land revealed to us by our dreams as the land of souls."

The lovely maiden heard the words of the Nanticoke, and answered that she knew not well what she should say. She knew not where the land of the Nanticokes lay, nor did she know who was he that spoke to her. But she timidly confessed that she loved him, and would become the wife of his bosom, if the consent of her father and mother could be obtained. So he asked the mother, who gave her consent at once, if that of her husband could be procured.

When the Sun came home at night, his wife said to him, "One of the six Indians that dropped from the North Star, on the shores of the Great Lake in the Frog-Moon, has come hither, and demanded our daughter Atahensic in marriage. He appears to be a bold and handsome youth, and our daughter loves him."

"But he shall not have her," answered the fiery father; "the blood of the Sun shall not mingle with the blood of the beings of the earth."

Then he called the Nanticoke to him, and spoke to him thus: "Thou canst not have my daughter—thy blood cannot mingle with mine.—Depart."

The Nanticoke, who, like all the others of that tribe, was brave and fearless, but prudent, held his peace, but departed not. When the Sun was asleep he wooed the maiden; when he was awake, and his eyes were peering into every spot however obscure, and every dingle however dark, he hid himself where even those rays could not penetrate. And often was the beautiful maiden of his love prevailed upon to hide herself with him. But he had suffered himself to forget the consequences of a mutual and unrestrained love. The beautiful Atahensic gave evidence that she should in due time become a mother. The quick-eyed father soon discovered what had happened, and heard the whole from the lips of his weeping daughter. Nothing could equal the rage of the mighty king of the skies, when he learned the disgrace inflicted upon his family. In the frenzy of the moment, he seized both the daughter and her lover, and hurled them from the highest part of the skies to the region where the land of the Nanticokes lay. But the kind mother protected both from the consequences of the fall, and the earth, by her command, received them unhurt upon her lap. Brothers, I am that Nanticoke, and the beautiful Atahensic is the woman by my side, and the child at her feet is the child of our love. I have no more to say.

When the first Nanticoke had finished his story, the second, whose name was Conestogo, rose, and thus addressed his brothers:

Listen, said he, and you shall hear of what befel Conestogo, who left you to travel into the bowels of the earth.

When he parted from his five brothers, he went to the deep cavern which lies among the mountains west of the river of the Nanticokes, and into this cavern he entered at the time of nightfall. After having groped his way for many days through deep darkness, over rocks and many other obstructions, living on the dried meat he had taken with him, all at once, upon passing through a small door or opening, he came to a great chamber, vaulted like the rooms which are unfolded to our eyes, when we enter those great houses in the City of the Rock, where men dressed in glittering robes, and little boys clothed in white, call upon the Great Spirit, and sing loud songs to his praise. Around the sides of this great room were tall pillars, which looked liked icicles, and glittered like them when they are visited by the beams of the sun. Over-head was a vast field of ice, of many different colours, green, red, white, yellow; the reflection of which on the floor of the mighty building occasioned a strange blending of rays. Beautiful, wonderful, was the appearance of this room, and of all within it.

But the most beautiful, wonderful things of the cavern remain to be spoken of. In the further corner of this spacious apartment was a company of beautiful maidens, clothed in robes of the same colours as those which glittered on the roof and walls of the building; the dazzling beauty of their dress may be guessed, but who shall paint their own charms? who shall describe their bright black eyes, long black locks, and voice like the music of the streams in spring? their beautiful necks, and little feet and hands, their swelling bosoms, and graceful footsteps? When I entered they were employed in chasing each other around the apartment, and amongst the lofty pillars; but, when they saw a stranger invade their retirement, they uttered a shrill cry of terror, and fled along the vaulted passages. The Nanticoke pursued them until he came to an inner range of apartments, all glittering like that he had left, but smaller in dimensions; there were a great many little recesses, and behind those pillars he saw many little heads peering out, which he knew to be those of the beautiful maidens who had escaped from the room of mighty pillars. He could see upon their countenances that they were not so fearful as they pretended to be; but when they hid, always preferred to be found. There was an arch smile upon their beautiful little faces, and their red lips were pursed up in affected contempt of the Nanticoke. He, whom nature quickly taught the best means of winning woman's love, which was not to seem over-anxious to obtain it, said nothing; but, seating himself upon a broken pillar, leisurely drew out his pipe and fell to smoking, rightly judging that if the fair creatures were not sought they would seek. It was not long that they remained hidden. First one contrived to put forth her little hand or foot; then a head became visible; still the Nanticoke affected to see neither. At last, finding that Conestogo would not play their childish game, one stepped forth, then another, and soon the whole stood visible. They now came up to the hunter, and, with many soft smiles, bade him welcome. Seating themselves upon the smooth floor around him, they commenced asking questions. "Who was he? what was he? how old was he? where did he come from? how far was he going? who was his father? what was the name of his mother? how many brothers had he? how many sisters? was his grandmother living? how long would he stay with them? to what place would he go when he left them?" and many other questions, which, fortunately for him, were asked with so little pause, that he had no opportunity to answer one of them. Nor did they seem to expect an answer, but appeared to ask, only that they might have the pleasure of talking. All were not so talkative, however. There was one beautiful creature, the most beautiful of all the company, who sat apart from the rest, said nothing with her tongue, but spoke a language with her downcast eyes, which the smitten Nanticoke interpreted into that of bashful love. While the rest were talking and laughing, displaying their white teeth, and shaking their black hair over their polished foreheads, he was thinking only of the silent woman, and contrasting her modest and quiet deportment with the noisy and boisterous mirth of her sisters. When she saw that the stranger bent his eyes a great portion of the time on herself, and that their expression denoted the same sentiment in him as filled her own bosom, she turned her face away to fix them in listless gaze upon a distant object.

After the beautiful maidens had laughed, and chattered, and questioned, as much as they would, they left the Nanticoke to enjoy his slumbers. The silent maiden retired last, and the look which she gave him, as she left the little chamber, did not quit his soul till more than half of the hours of darkness had run through. The next morning he rose early, and wandered about till he came to a little spring, which rattled over a bed of pebbles, and fell into a cavern beneath; it was a beautiful little spring, and its waters were cold and sweet, and as clear as the sky. He had just placed himself by the side of this little stream, when the silent maiden came thither also. The Nanticoke sat hidden from observation by one of the pillars, while she whispered her soft tale of love to the echoes of the cavern. She told them that she loved the stranger with the black hair, and sunny eyes, and proud mien; that she wished them to carry to the Great Spirit her wishes that he should ask her to become his own—his companion—his wife. More she would have said, but the Nanticoke caught her gently in his arms, preventing her slight screams with the kiss of love. "Thou shalt become my own—my companion—my wife," said he. "Lovely, and gentle, and dearly beloved creature! I had feared thou hadst no tongue, because to hear thee silent for a little while was something so new and strange in thy sex. But thou hast found a tongue to tell the echoes what thy bashful lips would not have dared tell me. I thank the Great Spirit that I overheard thy soft confession; it has removed those impediments which thy bashful timidity would else have interposed to our immediate union. Lovely maiden! with the black hair, and the bright forehead, and the slender waist, and the beautiful hand and foot, and the white teeth, what prevents thy accompanying me at once—to-day—this minute, to the land where I have taken up my abode, the pleasant and fruitful land of the Nanticokes? Again thou art silent, but the soft smile upon thy features tells me that thou art not averse to my proposal. I see in the look of thy sunny eye, in thy decreasing hesitation, and yielding reluctance, that thou wilt become the star of my pleasant cabin, the hope, the solace, and the joy of my life. Let us go then; ere ten suns be passed, thou shalt find thyself seated upon a bank, whose flowers are only less sweet than thyself. Thou shalt listen to a stream whose voice is only less musical than thine own, and see the beautiful night lit up by its very many glorious lamps.

"Brothers, I am that Nanticoke, and the beautiful maiden is she that sits by my side, and the child that rolls about on the green sod is the child of our love. I have no more to say."

The story of the second Nanticoke being finished, the third, whose name was Appomattox, rose, and thus addressed his brothers:—

Listen, said he, and you shall hear what befel Appomattox, who left you to travel eastward.

When he parted from his five brothers, he crossed the Great Arm [4] of the Salt Lake, and, in consequence of the revelations made by the spirit of a dream, pursued his journey towards the land of the cold spring-storms. He travelled fast, till he had wearied himself out, and then, building a small hut of bark to protect him from the rains and night-dews, he laid himself down to repose. He had not slept long, for the moon, that was a far way up when he sunk to sleep, had not reached the highest part of the heavens, when he heard a voice crying, "Appomattox! Appomattox!"

"Here I am," answered the Nanticoke. As he spoke, he raised himself up from his couch of leaves, and saw standing at his feet a strange-looking creature, whom the beams of the moon revealed to be a little, ugly, squat, brown man, not much higher than an Indian's hip. His shape was odd and singular, beyond anything the Nanticoke had ever seen. His legs were each as large as his body, and his feet were quite as much out of proportion. But his arms and hands were not larger than the arms and hands of the child which is playing at my feet, and his head was of the size of the head of a small dog, and similarly shaped. His eyes were red as the leaf of the maple in autumn; his skin was green as the bosom of the meadow in spring; yellow hair, as coarse as rock-moss, fell over his shoulders; and his nose was turned up till it reached his forehead; his ears were scarce larger than a man's thumb-nail, and his mouth than the blade of a pipe. It would have been a matter of wonder with the Nanticoke, how he could get the victuals into such a little mouth, if he had not been employed in noting the odd actions of the strange creature, and in listening to the tones of his voice, which resembled those of a cat when you tread upon its tail.

"Who are you!" asked the strange creature, and then gave a jump, turning himself head over heels, and stood upon his feet as before.

"I am a Nanticoke—one of the six who found themselves, in the morning of a clear day, in the Frog-Moon, standing upon the shores of the Great Lake, in the country where we have built cabins, and planted corn and tobacco. We know not how we were carried thither. We were, when we first knew we were—that is all we know. And who are you?"

"And that is as much as anybody knows," squeaked, or rather snarled, the strange creature, and again he took his tumble. "Wherever you came from, you seem a fine fellow, and I don't doubt wish for a wife. Come, go home with me. I live in a cave, in the hill close by, and will give you some fine fat toads, stewed with greens, for supper—or, if you like better, you shall have a roasted rabbit. As to who I am, I don't know myself. I only know that I am an odd sort of a fish."

The Nanticoke, who had not tasted food for many days, liked the offer of the rabbit very well, though he felt no relish for the stewed toads. So he went home with the strange creature to his dwelling in the hill. When they came to the the door of the cabin, the creature gave a knock with his foot, when the door was opened by a creature, stranger, if possible, than that which had conducted him to the cave. Upon entering, he beheld, scattered about the floor, a great many little children, quite as ugly and misshapen as the parents. Here lay one with a large leg and a little one, a full arm and a shrunken one, one-handed, or one-footed, or one-eyed. One had no hair: one was completely enveloped in it—in truth, the shapes were most various and singular. But all were not thus. Upon a bench, upon one side of the cave, sat a very little maiden—ye see how very little, and ye see how beautiful. When the Nanticoke entered, she drew her furred mantle around her, and pretended to hide her face, but she hid not her eyes, which were bent on the stranger youth. He had seen enough of her countenance to judge that she was very beautiful, and he loved her slight form, which he saw was light and graceful as the young fawn. He now entered into conversation with the old man, and they talked of many matters—he conversing quite like a sensible man, except that now and then he would take his strange tumble. At length, victuals were placed before them, and they sat down. The beautiful little maiden—with the usual pride of woman—dressed herself, and her black locks, with much care, and then came and placed herself at the table at which they were eating. Soft and fond glances were interchanged; and, before they had finished their meal, each had as good as said "I love." When they had done eating, the old man and woman arose, and under some pretence or other left the room, carrying with them the whole brood of odd and beast-like creatures. So the Nanticoke was left alone with the beautiful little maiden, to press her soft little hand, and to say in her ears those affectionate things which are always held sweeter by lovers for being told in whispers. Not much persuasion was necessary to obtain her consent to leave her father's house, and go with Appomattox to the spot where he had taken up his abode—to the cabin he had built beside the beautiful river Nanticoke. Their journey thither was not long—upon the sixth sun, they sat down upon the little plat of grass before the door of the cabin, and plucked the ripe grapes from the vines that leant upon its roof, and drank of the crystal stream which rattled over the pebbly bottom to the gentle river, and gathered the delicious berries that hung on every bush. And they saw the glorious sun illumine the earth, and the moon and stars lighting up the night, and the northern skies red with the dance of departed friends, and both blessed the moment that carried the Nanticoke to the hut of the very odd fish.

Brothers, I am that Nanticoke; and the beautiful little creature is she that sits at my side, and the little child that rolls about on the grass is the child of our love. My story is told.

And then the fourth Nanticoke rose, and told his story in the following words:

When I left my five brothers, said he, I crossed the river that glides by my cabin, and travelled towards the mountains which are called by Indians the Backbone of the Great Spirit. Upon the sixth day, I came to the hither part of the mountain, and sat down upon its eastern edge to rest my wearied limbs. It was near the hour of evening; the sun had not retired from the earth, but the lofty peaks of the mountains hid his beams from those who sat in the shade of those peaks, making it night to them. At length the sun set, and a thick veil of darkness was cast over the face of the earth. The ugly bat came forth, the mournful night-bird began his song, the wise owl hooted on the limb of the tree, and the dazzling little fire-fly twinkled in the glades, and among the trunks of the giant oaks. Then it was that a distant sound of music came to the ears of Apaumax the Nanticoke, who is myself. He listened, and caught the words, of a song issuing from a valley near the hillock upon which he sate. Softer than the plaintive cry of the dove, sweeter than the love-notes of the song-sparrow, was that song. Presently other voices could be heard laughing or singing, singly, or in concert. The Nanticoke was so greatly charmed with those notes that he determined to know whence they issued, and whose were the voices that sang them. So, descending the hill, he approached cautiously the spot where he had heard them, until he came suddenly upon a company of strange women who were dancing upon a green spot in the valley. They were the greater part of them very small, many being not taller than the sprout of three moons; but there were others, whose stature arose to the height of a full-grown person. Of the latter there was one whom the whole seemed to obey, the tallest woman of the group, and the most beautiful. She did not seem very youthful; at least her features spoke not of youth, nor did they imply age, but the period of life when woman is like a ripe grape, the sweetness of which is diminished by being suffered to hang a single day more on the vine untasted. She had a pale skin—ye see how pale—her cheeks were red as the flower that blooms among thorns, and her eye shone like the little flower which emulates the blue of the sky. Her lips were red and pouting, and her teeth whiter than the lily. Beautiful creature! lovely and beloved woman!

Cautiously did the Nanticoke approach the merry dancers, and, seating himself upon the earth where they could not observe him, he watched their sprightly and rapid motions. Nothing could exceed the beauty of the dances, or the grace of the dancers, or the sweetness of the tunes to which they danced. At last, one of the little maidens, in a fit of frolic, ran out of the circle of dancers, and by chance came to the spot where the Nanticoke had seated himself; a loud scream told him that he was discovered. When they found that a stranger had hidden near them, and witnessed their mystic dances, they were filled with great wrath, and all, as one, rushed up to the spot where he had concealed himself. He, knowing no fear, stood up boldly amongst them, and suffered them to scrutinize his person, rightly judging that nothing would so soon mollify their anger as to look upon his handsome and finely proportioned form. When they had gazed as much as they liked, she, the tallest, the one whom all obeyed, spoke in a stern voice, and asked, why he had dared to steal upon them while they were dancing the Sacred Dance of Darkness, and singing the Spirit's Song of Midnight? Did he not know that they were Spirits, the Spirits of the Mountain, who, for many hundred years, had nightly come, while summer lasted, to this green spot, to hold their joyous carousals, mixing music with mirth, and drinking the sweet drink which they found in the cups of the flowers and mottling the leaves of the rose. What had he to say why death should not be inflicted upon him?

The Nanticoke answered that he had much to say why death should not be inflicted upon him; that, having heard tones sweeter than those of the mocking-bird, and wishing to see who they were that laughed so merrily, and sung so sweetly, he had approached cautiously for that purpose. When he beheld the most beautiful creatures of the earth or the air engaged in dancing, and heard them singing their sweet songs, he was struck with wonder, astonishment, and admiration; and, fearing lest his discovering himself should frighten them away, he had hidden himself. This was all the crime he had committed. And, as for punishment, rather than die he was content to take the tall young woman to wife.

Upon this the spirits all laughed, except the one thus singled out, and she held down her head, though apparently not displeased. The Nanticoke, emboldened by her silence, whispered in her ear that he loved her; and, notwithstanding that her manner was at first repulsive, and she pretended to be displeased, and to frown upon the confident Apaumax, he could perceive that she had not suffered his words to fall to the ground. At first her face was averted, presently he caught a view of her mouth, and at last her face was actually turned towards him, and she was smiling bashfully upon the bold lover. Before the moon had advanced to the highest part of the heavens, they had given each other the kiss of love, and she had promised the Nanticoke to leave the cold regions of the mountain, and to go with him to his own sunny clime.

Brothers, I am that Nanticoke, and the tall, beautiful woman is she that sits at my side, and the child that is playing at my feet is the child of our love.

When Apaumax had finished his story, the fifth Nanticoke, whose name dwells not in my memory, rose and said:

When I left my five brothers, I went according to my agreement with them to the land of the warm sun, the smiling south. I travelled many days, and became hungry, faint, and weary. I saw no beasts upon which I could exercise my bow, no fish gliding about the waters, provoking the thrust of my spear. Here and there were scattered a few birds, but they were those upon which none can afford to feed, but a very patient man, or one that has nothing to do but eat. So, finding a pleasant resting-place, I lay down, and tried to call to my aid the Good Spirit, that refreshes the soul of man with pleasant dreams. He came and bade me arise with the morning sun, and travel further on, following the bend of the little river, at whose source I stood. I should come, he said, to a little hill upon the banks of a lake, filled with shining fish, and not far from the Great River. And, so saying, he left me to the sleep of night.

I rose refreshed by my slumbers, and pursued the route pointed out by the Spirit. Travelling in this path, I came on the morning of the next day to a little hill on the backs of a lake, and saw in its clear current the shining fish which had been spoken of by the spirit of dreams, and by this I knew that I had travelled right. The hill was a very little hill, and the lake was a very little lake, and the fish were very little fish. The hill was scarce half so high as the flight of an arrow; the lake was not broader than twice the flight of the same, when impelled by a vigorous arm; and the fishes were minnows indeed. Upon either side of the lake arose tall trees, around which grape-vines had wreathed themselves, and upon which fruit, ripe, black, and delicious, hung temptingly exposed to the eye of the traveller. The birds were twittering about the boughs, and swallows were skimming the bosom of the lake. But what most astonished the Nanticoke was, the great number of little cabins scattered along its shores. They were none of them higher than his hip, and were built of mud and grass. The Nanticoke, who loved to look upon the fair things of nature, the sun, and moon, and stars, and leafy woods, and green meads, and quiet waters, and other beautiful things of nature, sat down upon the border of the lake, and permitted the throb of delight to enter his bosom, through the medium of his eyes. While he sate thus absorbed, he saw a little black creature, with four legs, creep out of the water near him, and stretch itself at its length upon the green sod. It was black, glossy, and not longer than a man's arm. While it was devouring its food, which in this instance was roots dug from the marsh, it raised itself upon its two hind legs, to an upright posture, sitting erect as a Nanticoke, until it had finished. During the time it was eating, it was continually talking and chattering to itself, in a language, which the Nanticoke could discover, by the few words which reached his ear, to be that in which he himself spoke. Astonished, beyond the power of words to express, at hearing a beast speak, a beast, too, of such a mean appearance, he rose and advanced towards it. When it saw him coming, instead of retreating to the water, as beasts which are untamed usually do at the approach of man, whom all inferior creatures thus acknowledge as their chief, it advanced to meet him, made the sign of friendship in use among the Nanticokes, and spoke to him thus:

"Stranger! I bid thee welcome to the waters of the Lake of Musk-rats. Thou hast come to a region, rich in sunny skies, and yielding abundance of fruit. Thou hast come to the great village of my race, to the spot where we have dwelt ever since ourselves, and this lake, and that hill, were formed at the nod of the Great Spirit. Hitherto we have dwelt in peace, unvisited by one of thy race, but reason, and instinct alike inform me that thou wilt become the enemy of my tribe. Hitherto we have dwelt in peace, with none to vex us, or make us afraid—that period is past, and now thou wilt destroy us, unless something is done to unite us in the bonds of firm friendship. Thou hast proclaimed thyself a Nanticoke—one of the six that found themselves sitting upon the shores of the Great Lake, in the latter part of a warm and pleasant day, in the Moon in which the shad leave the waters that are salt, and journey to those that are fresh. It is well. Thou must be joined with the nation of Musk-rats in a lasting league. Come to my cabin."

So saying, the grave old Musk-rat led the Nanticoke to his dwelling, which stood at the farther part of the lake. It was built like the rest of the cabins in the village, but it was very much larger and handsomer than the rest, and there were a great many doors to it, and little houses around it, all of which showed it to be the residence of a Musk-rat of honour and eminence, a chief of high degree among his people. The chief of the Musk-rats bade the Nanticoke enter this cabin, but a moment after he said, "No, no, that cannot be done. It is not high enough for such a tall, strapping gawky as you are. So sit you here, while I go and fetch you food." So the Nanticoke seated himself on the sward, while the chief of the Musk-rats went to his house to fetch food for his guest.

He soon returned, and brought with him a variety of things to eat, which he placed on the sward, beside the Nanticoke. Some were such things as men may well eat, and some were only fit for a Musk-rat. The Nanticoke drew out his flint, and struck fire, while the chief of the Muskrats, who had never seen fire before, sat looking on and expressing loud amazement. After they had finished the meal, the chief gave a loud cry, upon which a number of little Musk-rats ran out of the house, and approached the spot where they were sitting. They were of all sizes, fat, sleek, glossy, little things, which seemed to delight in the pure air, and to enjoy greatly a roll about on the grassy sod. Approaching the Nanticoke, those which were old enough, with a very pretty nod, bade him welcome to the village of the Musk-rats—which showed that they had been taught good manners, though they were four-legged creatures. Shortly after, a beautiful Musk-rat was observed to leave the cabin of the chief, and to approach them circuitously. It came timidly, the beautiful creature, and sat down at a short distance from them. The chief of the Musk-rats upon this spoke to the Nanticoke, and asked him what he thought of his little daughter. The Nanticoke who, like all other good and brave men, always spoke the truth, answered that "she was indeed a most beautiful Muskrat—what a pity that she was still a Muskrat!"

"True, but she is the finest Muskrat in the waters of the lake," answered the father; "and she knows better than any other the best method of keeping a house tidy. And as for her knowledge—Musk-rat knowledge—who has more? and for cunning and stratagem, match me my little daughter among all the females of the lakes. What say you to marrying her?"

"All you have said in praise of your daughter, no doubt, is very true," answered the Nanticoke, "but she has four legs, and besides is too little to be the wife of a big fellow like myself."

"She has no more legs than you have," answered the wise creature. "What are your arms pray, but legs? But all her faults can be remedied. Wait here till I return."

So saying, the chief of the Musk-rats retired behind a little hillock, and, digging a small hole in the earth, he filled it with a kind of red sand mixed with mud. When he had done this, he dropped into it seven drops of a kind of green water, and seven times repeated the word "Tuscaloosa," which was, as he said, the name of the guardian Spirit of the Musk-rats. When he had done invoking the name, he laid himself down upon the earth, hid his head between his paws, and his tail between his legs, and pretended to be sleeping. Presently, the Nanticoke saw arise from the bottom of the lake a creature shaped like a Musk-rat, but larger than any beast he had ever seen. Each of his legs was as large as a tree, and his tail was broader than the length of a man, and his ears were of great size. He had a great white ring around his neck, and around each leg, and his belly was as red as the leaf of the maple in autumn. But the most singular things about him were his face, which was like the face of a man, and his fore-paws, which were like the hands of a man. The strange creature, who was the guardian Spirit of the nation of Musk-rats, came swimming along as a frog swims, and in scarce more than two breaths landed upon the shore where they sat. Going up to the chief of the Musk-rats, he gave him a slight blow on the back, exclaiming:

"What is your wish?"

"Take away from my daughter the shape of a Musk-rat, and give her the shape of a Nanticoke," answered the father.

"Not of me, but of my master must the favour be asked," answered the Spirit. "I will try what can be done for you." So saying, he went to the side of the little maiden Musk-rat, and whispered certain words in her ear. When he had done this, he went to the forest near them, cut down a young pine-tree, dug up a root of the hemlock, took a spruce cone, an oak acorn, a hickery nut, and a birch-leaf, and laid them all in the fire which the Nanticoke had kindled. While they were burning, he walked round the fire muttering many words in an unknown tongue, and striking the earth repeatedly with the stone staff which he held in his hand. When the different things he had put in the fire were reduced to ashes, he gathered the ashes into the hollow of his hand, dropped upon them seven drops of a kind of green water, and seven times cried aloud to his master, with his mouth applied to the ear of the earth. Ere the echo of the last cry had died away among the hills, a little red man crept out of the hole which had been dug by the chief of the Musk-rats, and stood before them. He was shaped like a Nanticoke, but he was exceeding small. His face was very beautiful, his eyes shone like the blue of the sky, and his hair like the blush of sunset. When he came, all the Musk-rats, as well as the genius who presided over them, bowed themselves to the earth, and remained with their eyes hidden, while he addressed them thus:

"What would you with the Master of Life, Musk-rats, that you summon him from his house of shining stone, in the bowels of the earth, to smell the tainted breezes of the upper air?"

The Spirit told his master what was wanted by the Musk-rats. "It shall be done," said the kind and beneficent Master. "Man of the Six Nanticokes, who found themselves, all at once, they knew not how, nor by what means, sitting upon the shores of the Great Lake, upon a sunny day in the Frog-Moon, rise, take thy bride, and lead her to the border of the lake. When thou shalt come to the water, bid her dip her feet in the water, while thou, standing over her, shalt pronounce these words: "For the last time as a Musk-rat, for the first time as a woman. Go in a beast—come out a human being. In the name of the Master of Life, I command thee to wear no more the form of an animal, but to assume that shape which is appointed by Him to be the ruler, the head chief, the governor of all. This do, and thou shalt see the change that will come.""

The Master ceased speaking, and the Nanticoke did as he was bid. He took the glossy little maiden Musk-rat by the paw, led her to the border of the lake, and, while she dipped her feet in the water, he pronounced aloud the words: "For the last time as a Musk-rat, for the first time as a woman. Go in a beast—come out a human being. In the name of the Master of Life, I command thee to wear no more the form of an animal, but to assume that shape which is appointed by Him to be the ruler, the head chief, the governor of all."

Scarcely were the words spoken, when the change commenced upon the little animal. Her body was observed to be assuming the posture of a human being, gradually erecting itself, as a sapling, which has been bent to the earth, re-ascends to its upright position. When the little animal became erect, the skin began to fall from the head and neck, and gradually unveiling the body to the very feet, displayed to all around the form of a maiden, beautiful as the flowery mead, or the blue sky filled with stars, or the north, lit up by the dance of departed friends, or the rainbow, which precedes, or follows the summer rain; but not so large as the little child which stands at my feet. Her hand was scarce larger than a hazel-leaf, and her foot not longer than the wing of the ring-dove. Her arm was so very slight, that it seemed the breeze might break it. The Nanticoke gazed with delight on his beauteous bride, and how was his delight heightened when he saw that she was gradually increasing in stature, and swelling to the fair size and proportions of a human being, as exhibited in himself! Before the great star of day had retired beyond the mountains of the west, she stood fair in size as matchless in charms, and was pressed to the heart of the Nanticoke, with a suitable acknowledgment to the Great Being, who had bestowed her upon him.

Brothers, I am that Nanticoke, and the beautiful woman that was once a Musk-rat is she that sits at my side, and the child that is playing at my feet is the child of our love. And this is all I have to say.

The last of the Six Nanticokes commenced his story thus:

I left my brothers, and travelled towards the regions of cold and snow — the land of perpetual ice and frost. I travelled many, very many days, over hill and through dale, now encountering the keen air of the mountains, and now the damp fogs of the low grounds, when I came, at the hour of noon, to the bottom of a deep valley. In the bottom of this valley, was a well dug in the earth, and which appeared to have no bottom. It was half as wide over as the flight of an arrow, and how deep no one could say. The waters which met the eye at a vast distance below the surface of the earth were green as grass, and, what seemed most strange to those who saw them, appeared to be full of eyes, bright shining eyes, resembling what bubbles blown upon the water would be, if they could be lit up by the beams of the sun. And whether it was that there were winds uttering sounds in the well or not, could not be told, but certain it is that whispers proceeded therefrom like those of human voices, sounding in deep caves. Fatigued by my long journey, I lay down upon the earth by the side of the well, intending to sleep. But the spirit which presides over the night came not at my summoning, and I lay restless and discontented, until the moon had climbed the tops of the highest hills. Then it was that shapes of strange appearance, Spirits, which bore the likeness of human beings in all save their eyes, began to come out of the well. They were of all colours and sizes, tall, short, thick, spare, black, white, grey, green, yellow, red. But in colour the eyes of all were alike—all were bright, and shining, and glittering like the blush of sunset. There were both men and women, and there were also many children. As soon as the Spirits of the Well stood upon the earth, they immediately formed themselves into a circle, and began dancing. Lightly did they trip away on the green sod, dancing without intermission for the whole period between their first appearance on the earth and the first glimmer of day upon the tall peaks of the mountains. When the red tinge which announces the approach of the sun first appeared, they all stole into their hiding-place, and again were the waters of the well filled with eyes, resembling sun-lit bubbles, and again whispers proceeded therefrom like those of human voices sounding from deep caves.

The Nanticoke—that is myself—who was now burning with curiosity to know something more of the strange creatures dwelling in the well, determined to stay yet another night to accost them, and to learn who and what they were. So he built him a hut of bark near, and reposed beneath it, until the shadows of night again descended upon the earth. With the beam of the rising moon again ascended these merry dancers, the Spirits of the Well, and commenced their gambols on the green sod. But what most astonished him was, that on neither night had they spoken to him, or given indications that they considered him a living being. In performing their mazy dances, they had several times come within a few feet of him, and once one of the agile creatures, running out of the circle, cleared his head with a bound, which showed that the impediment was observed and avoided. Determined to make himself known to them, if words could do so, the Nanticoke, a stranger to fear, approaching the circle of dancers, thrust himself into the midst of them. Yet was his object unaccomplished. They danced around him, they crossed their hands touching him, they leaped over him, in appearance they ran against him, though he felt them not. Still none of the circumstances produced recognition. He hallooed, apparently they heard him not; he danced with them, they heeded not his motions. Determined, whatever it might cost him, to make them know him, he caught at a passing form, selecting, for the object of his embrace, the most beautiful of all the dancers, a lovely woman, whose beauties cannot be described. What did he embrace? A shadow! a mere phantom! That beautiful form is a shade! He draws not to his bosom a creature invested with the attributes of humanity, with its virtues, its faults, its weaknesses. He feels not the soft breath of woman fanning his cheek, nor the throb of her little heart bounding against his own. There comes a cold, clammy air to his brow, like that of water in a cold morning, and the pulsation of his heart is checked instead of quickened. She is gone. He finds he has no more power to retain her in his arms, or to awaken in her a knowledge of his existence, than he has to arrest the march of the summer wind, or to hold conversation with the stars of night. Another, and another, and yet another fruitless attempt to clasp that form, for whom he begins to feel a new, and strange, and predominating interest, convince him that they are not of his order, but exist unapproachable by beings of clay. Again the morning dawns, and again they fly to their damp and chill retreat.

The Nanticoke, exhausted by long watching, and wearied out by incessant exertion to embrace the beautiful phantom, lay down upon the earth, and sunk into a deep sleep. Then it was that the Manitou of Dreams came to his couch, and whispered in his ear these words:

"Nanticoke! the shadows which nightly appear to thee are the Spirits of the Well. In this well for many hundred years have they dwelt, and every night do they visit the upper air to respire its breezes. Unlike other spirits, they see not human beings, nor can they by any means, short of the direct interference of the Master of Life, be made sensible of their presence. Blows touch them not, nor do their eyes behold those things which mortals behold, but those which mortals behold not. They have a world of their own, which, though it be comprised within the space of the world we inhabit, is distinctly separate in its nature and properties, and requires things of a different order to inhabit it. They wear, as you see, the shape of a human being, but they have none of its properties save the shape.

"How shall I make myself known to them? how shall I make myself known to the beautiful creature I have so often tried to clasp in my arms?" demanded the Nanticoke.

"It is to tell thee how that I am now at thine ear," answered the Master of Dreams. "Listen."

"Peel from the vine that bears no fruit its inner bark, and of this twist thee a long cord that shall carry to the water of the well the thing thou shalt tie to it. When it is finished, attach to it the white flat stone having in it little shining specks, which thou shalt find lying upon the edge of the near rivulet, where the feet of deer have worn a deep and broad path. Thou must let this stone descend with a quick motion till it reach the water, the whilst crying aloud, 'Come forth, maiden spirit with the bright eyes, and assume the corporeal state which shall fit thee for becoming a resident of the upper earth. Quit the impalpable form thou didst wear in the world of thine own, and be flesh, and blood, and bones, and marrow, in ours. Be no more the cold and chilled inhabitant of a dark, damp, and murky well, but become a warm and impassioned woman. Awake to the joys and sorrows, and hopes and fears, and doubts and disappointments, and cares and anxieties, which belong to human life. Awake to the throbs of love, and the joys of maternity.'" So saying, the Spirit departed to the place of his rest in the land of dreams.

The Nanticoke arose, and did as he was bidden. He peeled from the vine that bore no fruit its inner bark, and with it he made a cord of sufficient length to reach the water of the well. He searched for the flat, white stone with little shining specks in it, and having found it he attached it to the cord, and let it descend with a quick motion till it reached the water. Whilst it was descending, he cried aloud, "Come forth, maiden spirit with the bright eyes, and assume the corporeal state of a human being. Quit the impalpable form thou didst wear in the world of thine own, and be flesh, and blood, and bones, and marrow, in ours. Be no more the cold and chilled inhabitant of a dark, damp, and murky well, but become a warm and impassioned woman. Awake to the joys and sorrows, and hopes and fears, and doubts and disappointments, and cares and anxieties, which belong to human life. Awake to the throbs of love, and the feelings of maternity."

Scarce had the words escaped from his lips, when, by a ray of light which beamed into the well, he saw her he loved, her whose beauteous form he had so often attempted to clasp to his breast, ascending. Now she rises, suspended as it were, by nothing, now she has gained the earth. Already has she felt the change which has come over her, already she knows herself invested with other feelings and properties than those which have accompanied her in the state which she has quitted. Sounds are ringing in her ears which never rang there till now; visions are before her eyes which are now awakened for the first time. The music of birds, and the hum of bees, and the rattling of the distant rill, and the sighing of the wind, greet her ear, and her eyes are made happy by all the bright things which the Great Being has placed in this glorious world. And, most of all the objects which meet her eye, does the form of the Nanticoke please and gratify her. Her beautiful cheek is covered with a blush, her eye grows mellower, and her heart beats with a new, and till now unfelt passion. Few minutes pass ere she is in his arms, and has given and received the kiss of affection. She has awoke to the feelings of humanity, her heart has felt the throb of love, her bosom has been pained by the fear that it may not be returned; and anxiety, and joy, and grief, and many of the other passions of human nature, have visited her bosom. Beautiful creature! she has blushed on the Nanticoke her consent to be his, she has whispered in his delighted ear her happiness and pleasure; and, while she sits on the green sod at his side, she lays her head on his shoulder, and sings a sweet song of happy lovers, in the language of the Nanticoke which has become her own. I recollect not the words of that song, but it came to the ears of the enraptured Indian as the first word of a little child to the ears of its mother.

Brothers! I am that Nanticoke, and the beautiful spirit is she that sits at my side, and the child at my feet is the child she bore me. And this is all I have to say.

VI. THE UNIVERSAL MOTHER.

Before the world existed, and before mountains, men, and animals, were created; while the sky was yet without a sun, ere the moon and stars were hung up for the lamps of darkness, the Great Being, who is alike the preserver and sustainer of the red man and his younger brother the white man, was with the woman, the beautiful spirit, the Universal Mother. This woman was not of the same nature as the Great Being. He was a spirit, bloodless, fleshless, bodiless; she bore the form, and was gifted with the properties of a human being.

At that time all was water, at least water covered all things. No eye could have discovered aught else, had there been an eye to see. That which existed was darkness—all was darkness—darkness.—Darkness was all, in all, and over all. There were no sounds abroad, no winds swept the face of the waters, which lay black, still, and stagnant, as the slime of a pool surrounded by a thick copse. The waters were rotted by their long continued stagnation, and the winds could not exist in the heavy and murky air.

Upon a certain time, this beautiful woman descended from heaven, till she came to the sleeping and stagnant waters. She was pregnant by the Great Being; and her immense proportions denoted that she would bring forth more than one. When she struck the waters, in her fall, she did not sink deep into them, but where she settled down, immediately land appeared, upon which she rested, and continued sitting. The land grew by degrees, and increased around her, so that in a short time there was so much spare room, that she could draw up her legs out of the water, in which they had hung for so long a time, that they were covered with grass, like logs which have been floating in the sea. And still wider grew the space of solid earth, like that which would appear when the water recedes from sand which it had previously covered. Gradually the land spread itself from the seat of the beautiful woman, until its extent was soon beyond the reach of the eye. And, as the land increased, the motion of the waves, from the rush of the new-born winds, threw it up into the heaps and piles which are the hills and mountains, leaving, along its low spaces, the waters, which are the rills and rivers of the earth.

While the woman sat thus, watching the growth of the earth, she perceived unusual appearances upon its surface. Grass and herbs began to appear; trees, both fruitful and unfruitful, sprang up; and, in a short time, all things proceeded, and grew as they now are. Soon was a robe of grass and flowers spread over the naked sod;

and soon, though not so soon, was it shadowed by a thick and al-most impervious forest. The pine, and the oak, and the walnut, and the spruce, and the hemlock, broke through the crust of the earth, and the inferior shrubs made themselves a way to the light of the air. Soon all things proceeded, and grew as they now are, and the world became the beautifully green, and verdant, and flourishing, world it is now.

When the earth had grown to its present size, and had become covered with grass, the beautiful woman, who had carried her bur-then in her womb for forty seasons, gave it to the light. She was delivered of three kinds of fruit. The first was like a deer, in every respect; the second had the shape of a bear; the third had the form and nature of a wolf. The woman nursed these fruits with great care and tenderness, until they had attained their full growth. Then she took all the three sons, or kinds of fruit, as husbands, living with each by turns. The result of this connexion or cohabitation was the production of other animals, always more than one at a birth, and from these sprung all the other animals of the various kinds and species to be seen at this day. In time, as well from natural instinct as suitableness, each associated, with its own kind and species, and has so continued to do ever since. But the connexion did not always produce progeny of the same nature and stock as the parents. Every production and re-production further diversified the animal race, until the almost infinite variety of creatures was produced. The dog was the son of the wolf, and the house-cat was the daughter of the panther; the teal was of the children of the grey goose; and who fathered the sparrow-hawk but the eagle?

When all things were properly disposed, and placed in a condi-tion to subsist, and to continue of themselves, the Universal Mother, having accomplished her designs, joyfully ascended to the sky which she had left. In the mean time, she told the Great Being what she had done. He said to her, "You have done well as far as you have done, but you have left undone one thing you ought to have done. You have created an innumerable number of beasts, but they are without a head. You ought to have made a being endowed with wisdom, to govern, with a little of my help, the affairs of the world, and to preserve its less important matters in some kind of order. The animals and creatures you have made are, many of them, great fools, and none very wise, and, besides, are without souls competent to receive instruction. There is not one of them that has understanding enough to direct the feet of his neighbour in the path he should go—it would be the blind leading the blind, and together would they fall into the ditch. What more would the bear do, if he were made ruler, than train his subjects to perform great feats of strength, or to climb a tree, or to suck their paws through the long nights of winter?—The panther would teach them savage cruelty and a speedy step, and the deer would counsel them to fly from the pursuit of a snail, or a land-tortoise, or the cry of a wren, or the prate of a jackdaw; the fox might teach them cunning, and the dog sagacity, and the wild cat nimbleness, and the antelope fleetness, and the wolf courage, and the owl an insight into my ways. But there must be a being to repress the insolence, and controul the rage, of the more savage creatures, and to protect, as far as he can, the weaker from the oppression of the stronger. Such a being must be created, and be called MAN. Descend, once more, to the earth, beautiful and Universal Mother! and give birth to one more being, who shall be the lord of all the creatures that live, move, or breathe, on the land, in the air, or in the water."

Upon receiving this command, the Universal Mother again descended to the earth. She selected for her husband, in order to the production of the new being, a very subtle owl, who was the half-brother of a bear and a wolf, the cousin of a dog and a deer, and distantly related to the panther, the fox, the eagle, and the adder. By him she had, at one birth, two children. Men take their qualities from the beasts, to whom they are related, and most from those of whose blood they have most in their veins. If they have most of their great father's, the owl, they are wise, and generally become priests; if the wolf predominates, they are bloody-minded; if the bear, they are dirty and sluggish, great eaters, and love to lick their fingers; if the deer, they are exceedingly timorous and feeble; if the fox, cruel and sly; the eagle, bold, daring, and courageous, and the adder, treacherous. Thus men have, all their different natures and properties from the brutes, and oftentimes are worse than brutes.

THE COMING OF MIQUON.

Will my brother listen? will he hear what a Mohegan has to say of the manner in which his nation first became acquainted with the white people?

A great many seasons ago, when men with a white skin had never been seen in the land of the Mohegans, before the Fire-eater had come to take the place of the Yagesho(1), or the pale-face had succeeded to the less destructive Mammoth(2); some men of our nation, who were out at a place where the sea widens, espied, far away on the bosom of the Great Lake, a very large creature floating on the water. It was such an object as they had never seen before. Fear of this creature immediately filling their bosoms, they hastily returned to the shore. Having apprised their countrymen of what they had seen, they pressed them to accompany them, and make further discoveries of its nature and its purpose in coming thither. Launching their canoes, they hurried out together, and saw with increased astonishment the wonderful object which was approaching. Their conjectures were very various as to what it was; some believed it to be a great fish, or animal; while others were of opinion that it was a very big house floating on the bosom of the Great Lake. They were not long in concluding that this wonderful and mysterious object was moving towards the land, and they also saw that it was endued with life. Deeming it proper to inform all their brethren, to whom intelligence could be conveyed, of what was coming, that they might be on their guard, they dispatched swift runners and fast rowers in every direction, to the east, west, and north, to carry the news to the scattered chiefs, and tribes, that they might gather their warriors together, and prepare to combat, if need were, the strange creature. Soon, the chiefs and warriors of the neighbouring tribes were collected in great numbers, at that part of the shore which the strange creature was clearly approaching. It soon came so near that they were able to make it out to be a large moving house, (though they had never beheld such) in which, as they supposed, the Great Spirit himself was present, and coming to visit them.

Wishing to receive him in a manner which should mark their sense of his goodness to them and their fathers, to the giver of the corn, and the meat, and the victory over their enemies, they deliberated in what manner that object could be best accomplished. The first thing was to provide plenty of meat for a sacrifice, and with this view the best hunters were dispatched to the forest, in quest of those animals supposed to be most acceptable to the mighty guest. The women were directed to prepare *tasmanane* and pottage in the best manner. All the idols were brought out, examined, and put in order. As a grand dance was always supposed to be an agreeable entertainment to the Great Spirit, one was ordered, not only for his gratification, but that it might, with the aid of a sacrifice, appease him, if he were angry with them, and induce him to stay his hand, rather than slay them. The priests and *powwows* were called, and set to work to determine, if possible, what this remarkable event portended, and what the possible result might be. They came habited in their robes of magic, skins of black bears, the head, nose, ears, teeth, as also the legs, with the long claws, appearing the same as when the animal lived, with a huge pair of buffalo-horns upon the head, and a large bushy tail projecting from behind. Some were frightfully painted, some had the skin of an owl drawn over their heads, and some had snakes wreathed around their bodies. To them, and to the chiefs and wise men of the nation, the women and children, and the men of inferior note, were looking up for advice and protection. And now, filling their gourds with water from the stump of a fallen cypress, they began their work of incantation, by muttering over the magic water a charm that had hitherto been of potent influence, and words that called upon many spirits to assist in effecting the wishes of the masters of the spell. The spirits answered not, and the priests became so distracted with fears at the unusual deafness of those who had given them their power, that they increased the fever of apprehension they should have assisted to calm. The gourds, with the charmed water, fell from their hands, and, though the dance was commenced with fervour and enthusiasm, yet, such was the alarm, that it did not possess the regularity and order with which the Great Spirit through songs, dances, and sacrifices, must be approached.

While in this situation, those men in canoes who had approached nearest to the strange object returned, and declared that it was a great house painted of various colours, and crowded with human beings. They thought it certain that it was the Great Spirit, bringing them some gift which they did not possess before. Other messengers soon arrived, who had seen the inhabitants of the house, and made a report which did not lessen their wonder, fear, or curiosity. They told their friends that they were men of a different colour from the Indians, and differently dressed; they were white as the flesh of a plucked bird, and wore no skins; and one of them, who must be the Great Spirit himself, was dressed entirely in red. The great house, or whatever it was, continued to approach. While approaching, some one in it cried to them in a loud voice, and in a language which they could not understand, yet they shouted in reply, according to the custom of the Mohegans. Much frightened at the strange voices, and at the still stranger creature which floated towards them, many proposed to retreat to the hills for security; others opposed this, lest offence should be given to their visiter, who would find them out and destroy them. At last, the strange creature, which they now found to be a great canoe, stopped, and, at once, the robes white as snow, which were spread over its numerous arms, and covered its three heads, fluttered in the winds like clouds in the season of ripe corn. Soon were many of the strange men employed in gathering these robes into folds, as Indians pack skins. Presently a canoe of smaller size approached the shore where the Indians sat, having in it the man who was dressed in red and many others. When he had landed, leaving his canoe with some of his men to guard it, he approached the Mohegan chiefs and warriors who were assembled in council, and had seated themselves in a circle, as is their custom when about to receive ambassadors and messengers of peace. The man in red walked fearlessly into the midst of them, and saluted them all with great kindness, taking a hand of each, which he shook very hard. The Indians, on their part, testified their gladness, and their friendship, and their emotions of joy and satisfaction at their arrival, by loud shouts, and by rubbing their cheeks against those of their new acquaintance, and by patting them on the back. Lost in admiration of the strangers, of their dress, so gay and so dissimilar to that of the Indians, their manners so unlike, their features so different, and their language so utterly unknown, the Mohegans could do nothing but wonder and applaud. A large portion of their admiration, was however, reserved for the man who wore the glittering red coat, and who, they doubted not, was the Great Spirit. The curiosity of the people was expressed in a thousand different ways; the priests wondered whether the Great Spirit knew and recognised them as old acquaintances; the warriors, whether the men who accompanied him were fleet, and courageous as themselves; and the women were very curious to know if the men were like our own men, and loudly expressed their determination to ascertain the fact. All agreed in this, that whether beings of this world, or of the land of dreams, they must be treated with great kindness(3), and fed upon the choicest viands of the tribe.

Meanwhile, a large hackhack, or gourd, was brought to the man in red by one of his servants, from which he poured an unknown liquor resembling rain-water, into a small cup of such an appearance as the Indians had never before seen. He drank the liquor from this cup, and, filling it again, he handed it to the Mohegan chief standing next him. The chief received it, smelt to it, and passed it untested to the chief standing by him, who did the same, till it had been handled and smelt to by all the Indians in the circle, while not one had tasted it. The man who last took the cup was upon the point of returning it to the supposed Manitou in red; when the Bender of the Pine Bow, one of the bravest Mohegans, and the stoutest warrior in the nation, rose and spoke to his brothers thus:

"It is not right for us to return the cup with its contents untested. It is handed to us by the Manitou, that we may drink as he has done. To follow his example will be pleasing to him; it will show our confidence in him, and the courage which we have been told is highly valued by him. To return the cup with its contents untasted, will give him reason to think that we believe it to be the juice of the poison-tree; it will provoke his anger and bring destruction upon us all. It is for the good of the nation that the contents of the cup should be swallowed, and, as no one else will do it, the Bender of the Pine Bow devotes himself to the killing draught. It is better that one man should perish than that a whole nation should be destroyed."

The Bender of the Pine Bow then took the glass, and, giving many directions, and bidding a solemn farewell to his family and friends, resolutely drank its fearful contents. Every eye was fixed upon the brave man, to see what effect the strange liquor would produce. Soon he began to stagger, to whine fearfully, to roll up the whites of his eyes, to loll out his tongue, to shout, and to act a thousand other extravagancies. At last, he fell prostrate on the ground, and a deep sleep came over him. His companions, supposing him dead, fell to bemoaning his fate, and his wife set up the death-howl; all thought him a martyr to his valour and his love for his nation. But the man in red only laughed at their grief, and by signs gave them to understand that he would rise again. He told them true: the chief awoke, and declared to his friends that he had enjoyed, while apparently lifeless, the most delicious sensations, and that he had never before felt so happy as after he had drunk the cup. He asked the stranger in red for more; his wish was granted: the other Indians made the same request, and so was theirs; the whole assembly tasted the contents of the cup, and all became as mad and intoxicated as their leader. Soon was the Mohegan camp a scene of noise and tumult, brawl and bloodshed.

After the general madness had ceased, the man in red and his associates, who, while it lasted, had confined themselves to their canoe, returned to the shore, and distributed presents, such as beads and axes, among the Indians. The two nations soon became familiar with each other, and a conversation ensued, wherein the wants and wishes of each, as far as they could be made intelligible, were conveyed by signs. The strangers gave them to understand that they must recross the Great Salt Lake, to the vales which contained their wives and little ones; but that they would be back again when the season of snows should have passed, and would bring with them more and richer presents. With these promises, they departed.

When the season of flowers came round again, it brought with it the man in red, and a great band of followers. The Indians were very glad to see the pale faces, who appeared equally pleased at the meeting. But the latter were much diverted, and made a great laugh at the uses to which the Indians had put their presents, for they had suspended the axes and hoes around their necks, and used the stockings for tobacco-pouches. The visiters now taught them the proper use of those implements. Having put handles to the axes and hoes, with the former they felled great trees, making the forest ring with their blows; with the latter they cut up the weeds which choked the maize. The various benefits conferred upon the Indians by their visiters confirmed them in the belief that they were indeed spiritual beings, he in red being in their estimation the Supreme Manitou, and his attendants, the inferior Manitous. The visiters did not this time all go back in the canoes; many of them continued to abide with the Indians, who gave or sold them land(4), and lived very contentedly with them until they wished to dispossess them of the very grounds where they had buried the bones of their fathers. Wars were then commenced, and the Indians were soon dispossessed of the soil which was theirs by their birthright.

NOTES.

(1) *The Yagesho.*—p. 99.

I have not the means of judging whether this is an imaginary beast or not, probably it was. The following is the Indian account: The Tagisho, or Yagesho, was an animal much superior to the largest bear, remarkably long-bodied, broad down by his shoulders, but thin or narrow just at its hind legs. It had a large head and fearful look. Its legs were short and thick; its paws (at the toes of which were nails or claws, nearly as long as an Indian's finger), spread very wide. It was almost bare of hair, except the hinder part of its legs, in which places the hair was very long. For this reason, the Indians gave it the name of *"Naked Bear."* Several of these animals had been destroyed by the Indians, but the one of which the following account is given, had escaped them, and for years had from time to time destroyed many Indians, particularly women and children when they were out in the woods gathering nuts, digging roots, or at work in the fields. Hunters, when overtaken by this animal, had no way of escaping, except where a river or lake was at hand, by plunging into it, and swimming out or down the stream to a great distance; when this was the case, and the beast was not able to pursue further, then he would set up such a roaring noise, that every Indian hearing it would tremble. This animal preyed on every beast he could lay hold of; he would catch and kill the largest bears and devour them; while bears were plenty, the Indians had not so much to dread from him; but, when this was not the case, he would run about the woods, searching for the track or scent of hunters, following them up, and making prey of them. The women were so afraid of going out to work, that the men assembled to deliberate on the manner or plan of killing him. At, or near a lake (Hoosink), whence the water flowed two ways, one on the northern and the other on the southern end, this beast had his residence, of which the Indians were well informed. A resolute party, well provided with bows, arrows, and spears, made towards the lake; on a high perpendicular rock they stationed themselves, climbing up this rock by means of Indian ladders, and then drawing these after them. After being well fixed, and having taken up a number of stones, they began to imitate the voices and cries of the various beasts of the woods, and even that of children, to decoy him thither. Having spent some days without success, a detached party took a stroll to some distance from the rock. Before they had reached the rock again, this beast had got scent, and was in full pursuit of them; yet they reached it before he arrived. When he came to it, he was in great anger, and sprung against it with his mouth wide open, grinning and seizing the flinty substance as if he would tear it to pieces. He had several times sprung nearly up. During all this time, numbers of arrows and stones were discharged at him, until his death was finally effected, and he dropped down and expired.

(2) *The Mammoth.* — p. 99.

"An Indian chief of the Delaware tribe, who visited the governor of Virginia, during the Revolution, informed him that it was a tradition handed down from their fathers, that in ancient times a herd of these tremendous animals came to the Big-bone Licks, and began a universal destruction of the bear, deer, elk, buffalo, and other animals, which had been created for the use of the Indians. The Great Man above, looking down and seeing this, was so enraged that he seized his lightning, descended on the earth, seated himself on a neighbouring mountain, on a rock, (on which his seat and the prints of his feet are to be seen to this day) and hurled his bolts among them, till the whole were slaughtered, except a big bull, who, presenting his forehead to the shafts, shook them off as they fell; but, missing one at length, it wounded him on the side, whereon, springing round, he bounded over the Ohio, the Wabash, and the Illinois, and finally over the great lakes, where he is living at this day." — *Jefferson's Notes on Virginia.*

(3) *White People treated with great kindness.* — p. 105.

In every instance the white people, on their first interview with the Indians, were treated well. Varrazano (see *Hakluyt's Voyages,* vol. ii, p. 295, 300, Lond. 1600.) upon his landing on the North American coast, (which was near Wilmington, North Carolina), found the natives very hospitable. "Great store of people," says he, "came to the sea side, and, seeing us approach, they fled away, and sometimes would stand still and look back, beholding us with great admiration; but afterwards, being animated and assured with signs that we made them, some of them came hard to the sea-side, seeming to rejoice much at the sight of us, and marvelling greatly at our apparel, shape, and whiteness; and shewed us, by sundry signs, where we might most commodiously come to land with our boat; offering us also of their victuals to eat." Again, at another place, one of the sailors who had landed with a few articles designed as presents, found himself treated in the kindest manner. "These guileless people conducted him to the shore, and held him some time in a close embrace, with great love, clapping him fast about, in order to evince their regret at parting."—*See Varrazano's Letter in Hakluyt, and New York Hist. Collect.*

The treatment experienced by Columbus was equally kind. When Americus Vesputius landed, he was treated as a superior Being; all the early voyagers, the Cabots, Jacques Cartier, Sir Humphry Gilbert, Hudson, speak of the unbounded kindness and hospitality they experienced from the Indians. In the first report of Sir Walter Raleigh's Captain, it is said that they were entertained with as much bounty as could possibly be devised. They found the people most gentle, loving, and faithful, void of all guile and treason, and such as live after the manner of the golden age.—*See Hakluyt.*

In the first sermon ever preached in New England, the preacher says of the Indians: "They have been to us like lambs, so kind, so submissive and trusty, as a man may truly say many Christians are not so kind and sincere. When we first came into this country, we were few, and many of us were sick, and many died by reason of the cold and wet, it being the depth of winter, and we having no houses nor shelter; yet, when there were not six able persons among us, and that they came daily to us by hundreds, with their sachems or kings, and might, in one hour, have made a dispatch of us, &c. yet they never offered us the least injury."—*Sermon* printed 1622, reprinted Bost. 1815.

(4) *Gave or sold them land.*—p. 99.

At Stoke Pogis, Buckinghamshire, the seat of John Penn, Esq. the grandson of the founder of Pennsylvania, is preserved a portion of the trunk of a tree, supported on a marble base. On a brass plate is this inscription:

"This part of the great elm, under which the treaty was held, A. D. 1681, between Penn and the first inhabitants of America, in the neighbourhood of Philadelphia, and which was blown down A. D. 1810, is a present from some of the Society of Friends or Quakers, residing in Pennsylvania."

It is added: "The tree was in some danger during the American war, while the British army was in possession of that city, it being often necessary to cut down the trees in its vicinity for firing. But the late General Simcoe, who had the command of the district in which it grew, was induced, by his esteem for the character of William Penn, and the history connected with it, to order a guard of British soldiers to protect it from the axe."

By the side are some portraits of the Indian chiefs who signed the following deed:

"This indenture witnesseth, that we, Packenah, Jaultham Jickals, Partsequolt, Jerois Essepimank, Felktroy, Hekellappace, Eromas, Macloah, Wissy Powy, Indian kings, sackmakers, right owners of all lands from Quing Quingus, called Duck Creek, all along by the west side of Delaware river, and so between the said creeks backwards as far as a man can ride in two days with a horse, for and in consideration of these following goods, and as paid in hand and secured by William Penn, proprietary and governor of the province of Pennsylvania and territories thereof; viz. 20 guns, 20 fathoms matchcoat, 20 fathoms stroud-water, 20 blankets, 20 kettles, 20 lbs. of powder, 100 bars of lead, 40 tomahawks, 100 knives, 40 pairs of stockings, 1 barrel of beer, 20 lbs. of red lead, 100 fathoms of wampum, 30 glass bottles, 30 pewter spoons, 100 awl-blades, 300 tobacco-pipes, 100 hands of tobacco, 20 tobacco-tongs, 20 steels, 300 flints, 30 pair of scissars, 30 combs, 60 looking-glasses, 200 needles, 1 skipple of salt, 30 lbs. of sugar, 8 gallons of molasses, 20 tobacco-boxes, 100 jews' harps, 20 hoes, 30 gimblets, 30 wooden screw boxes, 100 strings of beads; do hereby acknowledge, &c. &c. Given under our hand at Newcastle, 2d day of the 8th month, 1685."

The above is certified to be a true copy taken from the original, in Dec. 1813, by Ephraim Morton, of Washington, Pennsylvania, formerly a clerk in the land-office.

THE FUNERAL FIRE.

Once upon a time, many years ago, a war raged between the Chippewas and their enemies, and the lands of the hostile tribes were red with blood. It was then that a small party of the former nation encountered a band of the latter upon an open plain in the country of the Great Lakes. Meteewan, the leader of the Chippewas, was a brave and distinguished warrior; his martial deeds were the theme of every youth who looked to obtain renown in arms, and formed one of the principal subjects of discourse among the different tribes of the land. And never did the chief act with greater bravery, or more distinguish himself for prudence and personal prowess, than on this occasion. After he had, by the valour of his arm, turned the tide of battle against his enemies, and while he was giving the great shout of victory, he received an arrow in his breast, and fell dead upon the plain. No Indian warrior killed thus is ever buried. According to ancient custom, he was placed in a sitting posture upon the field of battle, his back supported by a tree, and his face turned towards the path in which their enemies had fled. His head-dress, with all its feathers and decorations, his martial equipments, his spear, and club, were accurately adjusted, and his bow and quiver leaned against his shoulder. In this posture his companions left him. A fate which appeared so evident to all proved deceptive however in the result. Although deprived of the power of utterance, and the ability to move, he heard distinctly all that had been said by his friends. He heard them lament his death without the power to contradict it; he heard them speak of his great deeds; he heard them depict the grief of his wife when she should be made acquainted with his fate. He felt the touch of their hands as they adjusted his posture, without the power to reciprocate it. His limbs, and all his faculties, except those of thought, were bound in chains of terrible strength, and he could not burst them. His thoughts flowed as freely as ever, but his limbs refused to second their commands. His anguish, when he felt himself thus abandoned, was raised to a dreadful height; but he was compelled to bear it, for no endeavours of his could allay it. His wish to follow his friends, who were about to return to their homes, so completely filled his mind, that, after making a violent exertion, he rose, or seemed to himself to rise and follow them. But he was invisible to them; they neither saw his form, nor heard his voice or steps, and this gave new cause for surprise. Astonishment, disappointment, rage, alternately filled his breast, while he attempted to make himself heard, seen, or felt, and found that he had lost the power to do either. He followed their track, however, with great diligence. Whereever they went, he went; when they walked, he walked; when they ran, he ran; when they encamped, he encamped; when they slept, he slept; when they awoke, he awoke. In short, he mingled in all their labours and toils; but he was excluded from all the sources of refreshment and enjoyment, except that of sleeping, and from participating in their conversation, for nothing, he said, was attended to. He saw them eat the sweet flesh of the deer, and the delicious dish compounded of corn and bison-meat, but no portion came to him; he saw them bend joyfully over the pleasant fire, which administered no reviving warmth to his shuddering limbs. He heard them recount their valiant deeds, but he was unable to tell them how much his own exceeded theirs; he heard them paint the joys which awaited their return to their homes, but wanted the power to say that he too had relatives and kindred not less loving and beloved than theirs.

"Is it possible," he exclaimed, with bitterness, "that you do not hear me—that you do not understand me? Will you suffer me to bleed to death without offering to stanch my wounds?—Will you give me no victuals to eat while your kettles are overflowing with the product of a fortunate hunt, and even the dogs are fed upon the savoury bison hump?—Have those whom I have so often led to war, so often enabled to cry the shrill cry of victory, and display the pole filled with scalps of hostile warriors, have they forgotten me?—Is there no one who recollects me, or who will offer me a morsel of food in my distress?—Am I indeed, as I fear, invisible to all?—Do I cease to wear the human form, and is my voice no longer a thing to be heard?" Thus he continued to upbraid his friends at every stage of the journey, but no one seemed to hear his words, or, if they heard his voice, they mistook its sound for the winds of summer rustling among the green leaves, and shaking the branches of the trees.

At length, the returning war-party reached their village, and their women and children came out, according to custom, to welcome their return, and proclaim their praises. *Kumaudjeewug! Kumaudjeewug! Kumaudjeewug!* they have met, fought, and conquered, was shouted from every mouth, and resounded through the most distant parts of the village. The aged warrior, whom weakness and decrepitude had compelled to throw down the bow and the spear, and the eagle-eyed boy, who was fast gaining upon the ripened period when he should take them up, did each his part in celebrating the feats which the one had equalled, and the other hoped to outdo. The wife, with a proud mien, came forward to meet the embraces of her renowned husband; the timid maiden, with a downcast eye, to steal a look at her valiant lover. Those who had lost friends came eagerly to enquire their fate, and to know whether they had died like men. The decrepid father consoled himself for the loss of his son with the reflection that he had fallen manfully, and the widow half forgot her sorrow amid the praises that were bestowed on the bravery of her departed husband. The breasts of the youths glowed with martial ardour as they heard these flattering praises, and children joined in the shouts of which they hardly knew the meaning, except that they related to the scalps suspended from the bloody pole. But, amidst all this uproar and bustle, no one seemed conscious of the presence of the wounded chief. He heard many inquiries about his own fate; he heard them say that he had fought, conquered, and fallen, pierced through his breast with an arrow, and that his body had been left among the slain.

"It is not true," replied the indignant chief, with a loud voice, "that I was killed and left upon the field—I am here. I live! I move!—See me! Touch me! I shall again raise my lance, and bend my bow in battle; I shall again sound my drum at the feast. My voice will again be tuned to sing my exploits in the ears of listening youth, and my arm raised to strike the painted post preparatory to the hostile incursion." But nobody seemed conscious of his presence, and they mistook the loudest tones of his voice for the mildest whispering of the winds. He now walked to his own lodge; he saw his wife within, tearing her hair, and raising her lamentations over his fate: he endeavoured to undeceive her, but she also seemed equally insensible to his presence or his voice: she sat in a despairing manner, with her head reclining upon her hands: he asked her to bind up his wounds, but she made no reply: he then placed his mouth close to her ear, and vociferated, "I am hungry, give me some food." The wife thought she heard a buzzing in her ear, and remarked it to one who sat near her. The enraged husband, now summoning all his strength, struck her a blow upon the forehead. She only complained of feeling a shooting pain there, such as is not unfrequent, and, raising her hand to her head, remarked, "I feel a slight head-ache."

Foiled thus in every attempt to make himself known, the warrior chief began to reflect upon what he had heard the priests and wise men say, that the spirit was sometimes permitted to leave the body, and wander about. He reflected that possibly his body had remained upon the field of battle, while his spirit only accompanied his returning companions. The part he had presented before the eyes of his apparently neglectful friends might have been that which mere human eyes see not. He determined to return upon their track, although it was four days' journey to the place. He accordingly began his immediately. For three days he pursued his way without meeting with any thing uncommon, but, on the fourth, towards evening, as he came to the skirts of the battle-field, he saw a fire in the path before him. He walked to one side of the path to avoid stepping into it, but the fire also changed its position, and was still before him. He then went in another direction, but the mysterious fire still crossed his path, and seemed to bar his entrance to the scene of conflict. In short, whichever way he took, the fire was still before him: no expedient seemed capable of eluding it. "Thou demon," he exclaimed at length, "why dost thou bar my approach to the field of battle, to the spot which contains my own inanimate body? Knowest thou not that I am a spirit also, and that I seek again to enter that body from which I have so lately been driven?—Or dost thou presume that I shall return without effecting my object because of thy opposition?—Know that I am a chief and a warrior, tried in many a hard battle, and never known to flinch. I have never been defeated by the enemies of my nation, and I will not be defeated by thee." So saying, he made a vigorous effort, and succeeded in forcing a passage through the flame. In this exertion he awoke from his trance, having lain eight days on the field of battle. He found himself sitting on the ground, with his back supported by a tree, and his bow leaning against his shoulder, having all his warlike dress and implements upon his body, the same as they had been left by his friends on the day of battle. Looking up, he beheld a large *canieu*, or war-eagle, sitting upon the tree above his head. He immediately recognised this bird to be the same he had dreamt of in his youth, and whom he had selected as his guardian spirit or personal Manitou. While his body had lain in its breathless and soulless state, this friendly bird had watched it, and prevented other ravenous birds from devouring it. He got up, and stood some time upon his feet, but he was weak and exhausted, and it was a long time before respiration became full and perfect, and the blood coursed in his veins as it was wont to do before its transient suspension. The blood upon his wound had stanched itself, and he now bound it up. Possessing, as every Indian does, the knowledge of such roots as were efficacious for its cure, he sought diligently in the woods for them, and obtained sufficient for his purpose. Some of them he pounded between stones and applied externally; others he chewed and swallowed. In a short time he found himself so much recovered as to be able to commence his journey, but he suffered greatly from hunger, not being able to see any large animals. With his bow and arrows, however, he killed small birds during the day, which he roasted before the fire at night. In this way he sustained himself, until he came to a water that separated his wife and friends from him. He then gave that peculiar whoop which indicates the safe return of an absent friend. The signal was instantly known, and a canoe dispatched to bring him across. But, while this canoe was absent, conjecture was exhausting itself in designating the unknown person who had given this friendly intimation of his approach. All who had been of the war-party had returned, except those who were killed on the field. There was no hunter absent. It might be a hunter of some neighbouring nation. It might be some deep deception or stratagem of their enemies. It was rash to send a canoe without knowing whether it was a friend or foe. In the height of these conjectures, the warrior chief was landed amidst the shouts of his friends and relations, who thronged from every lodge to welcome their faithful leader. When the first wild burst of joy and wonder had subsided, and some degree of quiet was restored in the village, he related to his people the account of his adventures which has been given. He then concluded his narration by telling them that it is pleasing to the spirit of a deceased person to have a fire built upon his grave for four nights after his interment; that it is four days' journey to the land appointed for the residence of the spirit; that, in its journey thither, the spirit stood in need of a fire every night at the place of its encampment; that, if the friends kindled this funeral fire upon the place where the body was deposited, the spirit had the benefit of its light and warmth in its sojourning; but, if they neglected this rite, the spirit would itself be subjected to the irksome task of building its own fire at night.

THE PORTIONING OF THE SONS.

The Great Being, who governs the world, having finished his work, and cheated every thing which is found upon the land, in the air, or in the water, called to him the red man, and his younger brother, the white man, and said to them, "Children, come hither." So saying, he carried them to a great pen or fold, upon one side of which stood a large coop, and on the other a big pond of water. In the pen or fold were a vast many animals, all four-legged, the deer, the bison, the horse, the cow, the panther, the musk-ox, the antelope, the goat, and the dog, with many more, such as the beaver, the otter, the mink, and the musk-rat, which lay with their tails in the pond and their heads in the pen; and others, such as the tortoise and the alligator, whose snouts preferred water, while their tails stuck to the land. In the coop were a vast many birds and fowls, some of beautiful and varied plumage, while others were robed in dirty and dingy feathers; some were very tender, and good to eat, and some were tough, and but so-so. I need not particularise the fishes, for my brother knows well enough what they are. When the young men had spent a long time in examining the animals, and birds, and fishes, admiring and praising them, as who would not that has never before seen them, the Great Creator addressed them thus:

"My sons, I have created many creatures, and breathed into them the breath of life; I have made the forests resound with the cry of bears, and panthers, and bisons; I have caused the air to be so thickly inhabited, that you can scarcely move without having your cheeks fanned by the breath of the wings of my birds; I have made the rivers populous with finny people. These—all things—I have created, are for your use, and to you two I give them, equally and alike." So saying, he began to divide the animals, and birds, and beasts, between them. To the red son, whom he loved best, because he was strong and feared nothing, he gave the beasts which partook of his own cunning and courage—the bear, the dog, the panther, the fox, and the beaver, to which he added for food, the deer, the elk, and the bison; to the pale-faced son he gave the horse to carry him, because his legs were weak, the cow, the hog, the sheep, and the cat. The white son took, of the feathered tribes, the fowl which crows at the glimmering of light, the duck and the goose, which love to dabble in mud, and the turkey, which sings a song that is none of the best; and the red man took the eagle, the owl, and all the rest of the birds. The fishes were not divided, because they could not be kept apart, but the sons agreed that the better marksman, the Indian, should prey upon those which called for a true aim with the spear, while the pale face should angle for those which required less skill, and were caught with less trouble.

When the division had taken place, as far as it was ever to take place, the white son took his gifts, and carried them carefully to a pleasant and clean field, where there was a bright sun, much water close at hand, and plenty of sweet and juicy grass. He then commenced the task of making his animals tame and tractable. He put pieces of trees across their necks, fastening them together by two and two, the cow and the horse, the hog and the sheep, the cat and the dog; but the hog pulled back so hard, and was so contrary, and the cat and the dog quarrelled so much and fought so furiously, that he unyoked the two last pair, and never attempted to make them work together again. With the horse and cow, however, which he found exceeding tractable, he succeeded in turning up the earth, for the planting of his corn, and his beans, and his pumpkins. He also made the cow serviceable, by obtaining a delicious drink from her udder, and he made the horse further valuable and useful by fixing a string to his mouth, and by throwing a bear-skin over his back, when, mounting him, he made him carry him whithersoever he would. The sheep gave him a soft down whereof he made his robes, and the blankets he sells to the Indians; the hog furnished him with meat; the dog helped him in many ways; but I know not to what use he put the cat. So the white son of the Great Spirit brought all his animals to be tame and useful, either making them afford him milk and meat, or help him to prepare the ground for the seeds he was commanded to plant therein.

My brother demands what did the red man with the gifts which were appointed to him. I will tell him. He looked on them very curiously for a minute, then wrapped them up loosely in his blanket, and laid them aside, intending to do with them the next day as his white brother had done with his. Just then the remembrance of something came across his mind, which led him astray from his purpose, and he thought no more of the blanket or the creatures which it contained, until many moons had passed away. When the remembrance of the imprisoned animals returned to his mind, he repaired to the spot where he had deposited them — nothing remained but the blanket. He immediately commenced a search for them, and found the pleasure and excitement so great and exhilarating, that ever since he has adopted this mode of obtaining his meat, instead of the method of raising tame animals followed by the foolish white men. It is still his favourite pursuit, and he no longer regrets his want of care, or wishes to repair his error. While the white man is doomed to hear the cackling of geese and the grunting of hogs, the lowing of kine and the bleating of sheep, and to watch over all and to tend all with the care and nursing which a mother bestows upon her helpless child, the red man with his arrows slung to his shoulder, and his mocassins tight-laced to his legs, escapes to the howl of the panther, and finds joy in the cry of the wolf. Over mountain, and through forest, goes the happy Indian, free as the air, while the white man is chained to his dull and spiritless pursuits, and fettered by his endless cares. The Great Being, doubtless, intended the Indian good when he made the apportionment of the creatures, but the Indian has never found fault with the incident which released him from the care of them, and gave him the pleasant occupation of hunting in lieu thereof.

THE MAIDEN'S ROCK.

If my brother has seen the River of Fish, he will know that, at the distance of a few moons' journey, below the rush of waters which the white man calls the Falls of St. Anthony, but which the Indians call the Island of Eagles [5], there is a beautiful lake, which the same people have named Lake Pepin. It is a place so beautiful to behold, that distant Indian nations have journeyed thither, and white people come from the city of Strong Walls, to look at it and admire. On one side lies the rapid Mississippi, now in foam, and now in eddies, sweeping every thing thrown upon its current with the rapidity that a man walks, and winding, in devious courses, among many islands, some of which are covered with lofty trees, and some are but banks of sand. On the other side lies the lake, which presents to the eye but a smooth sheet of water, on which there is neither wave nor ripple, and unchequered by a single island. As the eye passes along its sluggish surface, it rests at length upon the lofty bluffs which enclose it. One of these, a high projecting point, a precipitous crag resting upon a steep bank, whose base is washed away by the never-ceasing action of the waters, is called *The Maiden's Rock*. It is known to every Indian in those regions, by a gloomy story of unfortunate love. It was the scene of one of the most melancholy transactions that has ever occurred among our people.

There was once upon a time in the village of Keoxa, in the tribe of Wapasha, a young Indian woman, whose name was Winona, which means "the first-born." She was good and beautiful, and much beloved by all. She had conceived a strong attachment to a young hunter of her nation, who loved her as much as she loved him. They had frequently met, sometimes in the shady coverts of the wood, at others beneath the river's banks, but, according to the forms of Indian courtship, more frequently at the side of her couch, when all the village were at rest. They had confessed their love, and agreed to be united as soon as the consent of her family could be obtained. But, when he asked her of her parents, he was denied, and told that she was to become the wife of a warrior of distinction, who had sued for her. The warrior was a great favourite with the nation; he had acquired a distinguished name by the services he had rendered the village when it was attacked by the Chippewas; yet, notwithstanding all this, and the support which he received from her parents and brothers, Winona persisted in preferring the hunter. To all their loud commendations of the warrior, she replied that she loved another better; that she had made choice of a man, who, being a professed hunter, would spend his life with her, and secure to her comfort and subsistence, plenty of food, and abundant happiness: while the warrior would be constantly intent upon martial exploits, exposing her, if she staid at home, to the evils of want and hunger; if she accompanied him, to the dangers of defeat and death. Winona's expostulations were, however, of no avail; and her parents, having succeeded in driving away him she preferred to all the world, began to use harsh measures in order to compel her to marry the man of their choice. To all her entreaties that she might not be forced into a union with a man she did not love, they turned a deaf ear—to all her tears they were blind. She begged to be allowed to live a single life, and to spend her days watching the sleep, and preventing the cares, of her father and mother: they answered, No. Winona had at all times enjoyed a greater share in the affections of her family, and had been indulged more than is usual among Indian females. She had not been obliged to join in the labours of the field, nor in the more arduous of those within doors. She planted no corn, and the fire-wood and the buffalo's meat were brought home on other shoulders than hers. Being a favourite with her brothers, they expressed a wish that her consent to this union should be obtained by persuasive means, rather than that she should be compelled to it against her inclination. With a view to remove some of her objections, they took means to provide for her future maintenance, and presented to the warrior all that in their simple mode of life an Indian might covet. They furnished his cabin with the various implements used in Indian housewifery—the skins to form the bed, the boiling pot, and the roasting spit. About that time, a party was formed to ascend from the village to Lake Pepin, in order to lay in a store of the blue clay which is found upon its banks, and which is used by the Indians to adorn their persons. It was on the very day that they visited the lake that her brothers made their presents to the warrior. Encouraged by these fresh signs of their approbation, and inflamed by the beauties of the charming Indian girl, he again solicited her in the most passionate language to become his wife, but with the same ill success. Vexed at what they deemed an unjustifiable obstinacy on her part—for seldom does love among Indians urge to lengthened opposition on the part of the female—her parents remonstrated in strong language, and even used threats to compel her to obedience. They spoke, as parents always do, who have in view a husband to their liking, and care little for the peace and happiness of a daughter, so they see her possessed of what they covet. "Well," said Winona, "you will drive me to despair. I said I loved not the man of your choice, the warrior covered with the blood of peaceable women, and helpless children, and painted to resemble only those hideous things we see in sleep. I said I could not live with him and be his wife. I wished to remain a maiden—my father's daughter, and my brothers' sister—but you will not let me; you wish me to become a wife. You say you love me; that you are my father, my brothers, my relations, yet you have driven from my arms, and would now drive from my heart, the only man with whom I wish to be united—the only man I ever loved. You have persecuted him with wrongs; you have reviled and taunted him; you have compelled him to withdraw from the village. Alone, he now ranges through the gloomy and lonely forests, with no one to assist him, none to comfort him, none to spread his blanket, none to build his lodge, none to pound his corn. Yet, he was the man of my choice, the only beloved of my heart. Often have you taken me on your knee, and smoothed down my hair, and kissed my cheek, and said you loved me. Is this your love? But it appears that even this is not enough; you would have me do more—you would have me rejoice in the absence of my beautiful hunter. While yet his parting words are in my ear, the light of his eyes in remembrance beaming on me, and his tender promises all unforgotten, you wish me to unite with another man, with one whom I do not love, whose image comes before me but to make me weep and shudder. Since this is your love, let it be so; but soon you will have no daughter, sister, or relation, to torment with your false professions of friendship. I will go to the happy land of souls, where I shall be free from your threats and reproaches."

As she uttered these words, the canoe touched the shore in the immediate vicinity of the high precipitous crag of which a description has been before given. Heedless of her complaints, and wearied out with what they regarded as a most unreasonable repugnance, her parents at the moment decreed that Winona should that very day be united to the warrior. Her resolution was at once taken; it was such a one as could have been adopted only in a moment of deep love and deep despair. While all were engaged in busy preparations for the festival, she wound her way slowly to the top of the hill which overlooked the scene of their gay and mirthful doings. When she had reached the summit, boldly approaching the edge of the precipice, she called out with a loud voice to her friends below, upbraiding them with their cruelty to herself and her lover, and thanking the Good Spirit that had put it in her power to baffle their designs, and laugh at their tyranny. "You," said she, "were not satisfied with opposing my union with the man whom I had chosen; you endeavoured, by deceitful words, to make me faithless to him; but when you found me resolved to remain single, you dared to threaten me: you knew me not, if you thought that I could be terrified into obedience. Now, you are preparing the bridal feast, but you shall see how well I can defeat your designs." She then commenced a plaintive song of death, which ran thus:

Winona's Dirge.

Adieu to these green vales,
And to the pleasant shades,
Where oft I sate and listened to the song
Of birds at morn, and, in the evening hour,
To that which gives the alarm, and bids the band
Of Indian warriors grasp their spears.
No more my ears shall hear those sounds,
In this my father's land;
The notes of singing-birds shall pass me by,
And the soft sighing of the month of buds;
But I shall hear no howl of wolves,
Nor cry of famished bears,
Nor hissing of envenomed snakes,
Nor what more chills the heart,
The tyranny of father, brothers, friends.

Nor shall I be compelled
For ever to behold a hated face,
And shudder at the voice of him who sleeps
Beneath my blanket;
Nor, when within my cabin,
Young faces smile on old ones, shall I wish
Another eye looked on their beaming cheeks;
When the storms howl, I shall not think of one,
Alone in the far forest,
With none to spread his blanket,
With none to build his lodge—

Cold, hungry, lonely, in the desert glen.

But I shall cross the sharp and fearful rock,
And reach the dwelling-place of happy souls.
No deeds shall bar me out.
I never told a lie;
Kind have I been to father and to mother.
Returning from the hunt or field of war,
His daughter handed him a lighted pipe;
And she who gave her birth sat in the sun
Upon her bench, beside the lodge's door,
While young Winona baked the buffalo,
And drew the crystal water from the stream.

And I shall go where there is peace,
And where joy wakes for ever:
There I shall meet my hunter;
He shall build our lodge beside the murmuring stream,
And thatch it with the vine, whose ripe, black grapes
Shall hang adown in clusters;
Our little babes shall pluck them.
Warrior, I shall not be your wife —
Father, you have no daughter —
Brothers, your sister lies upon the earth,
Cold, bleeding, lifeless, and too late you mourn!

The light wind which blew at the time wafted the bitter words of her mournful dirge to the spot where her friends were. They immediately rushed, some towards the summit of the hill to stop her, others to the foot of the precipice to receive her in their arms, while all with tears in their eyes entreated her to desist from her fatal purpose. Her father promised her that no compulsive measures should be resorted to, that she should marry or not as, she chose. Her brothers, who loved her with great affection, urged every thing that they thought likely to be of avail, but in vain. She was resolved, and, as she concluded the words of her song, she threw herself from the precipice, and fell at their feet, a corpse.

EXPEDITION OF THE LENNI LENAPES.

The Lenni Lenapes, who are the grandfather of nations [6], were quietly reposing in their lodges on the banks of a shallow and noisy river, that finds an outlet in the mighty waters beyond the great mountains, and far, very far, towards the setting sun. If my brother would see this river; if he would behold the cataract that impedes the progress of the Indian canoe; if he would witness the strife that takes place when the waters that are fresh first mingle with those that are salt, let him call together his youngest and stoutest warriors, the nimble of foot, and strong of heart — the faint and failing, the old and trembling, the weak and cowardly, will not do, for the path is beset with savage beasts and strong warriors, and hostile spirits. Let him load his women with much provision, and make his mocassins of tanned bear-skin, for many are the suns it will take to journey thither, and rocky is the path that leads to that far abode. Mountains must be crossed, which are covered with snow, and upon whose summits the clouds break as the mist rises from the Oniagarah [7]. The warriors, who shall be seen in its path, will not bow down their heads to the axe of the stranger, till their spears are broken, and their quivers are bare of arrows. Nor then will they die like women, but with songs of past glory and present defiance in their mouths. And the spirits will not be appeased unless they have many offerings, and there will be in their paths the Dread Destroyer of Deer [8], he who laughed at the avenging arrow of the Master of Life, and is gone to prey upon the moose of the Lake of the Woods.

The Lenapes were living in their lodges, warring upon the Flatheads, feasting upon the salmon, and drinking the juice of the sacred bean [9], when it happened to one of their young warriors, that he dreamed a dream. Wangewaha, or the Hard Heart, though his years were but few, was one of the most celebrated chiefs of the nation. His days were but those of a young eagle; yet the bravest, even those who had watched the nut-tree from its sprout to its bloom, ranged themselves in battle under his faultless command, in the chase followed the ken of his eagle eye. He had struck more dead bodies, he had stolen more horses, he had taken more scalps, than any man of his nation. He could follow the trail of a glass snake from sun to sun, he could see the wake of a fish a fathom below the surface of the water. When he cast his eye upon a young maiden, she became his without a wrestle(1); when he told the revelations of the spirit of sleep, the aged men and wise councillors never called their truth in question, but acted upon them without reflection, believing them to be the voice of the Great Spirit, speaking through his favourite son. If he excelled in war and perilous pursuits, he excelled as much in those pastimes and games, wherewith the warrior in times of peace and rest beguiles the tedious hours. When Wangewaha struck the ball, its flight was above the soaring of the bird of morning, and he never rose from the game of bones(2) without giving proof that he was the favourite of heaven.

It was a beautiful night in the month in which the Indians gather their first green corn, when, as the chief lay sleeping on his bed of skins, with the mother of his youngest child on his arm, he saw strange things in his slumbers. He dreamed that the bands of the Lenni Lenapes had taken the bones of their fathers from the burying places of the nation, loaded their women with pemmican and dried corn, folded up their tents, and departed towards the regions of their great father, the sun. He saw mountains, whose summits breathed fire, and others, which were the abode of the snow spirit—now noisy with the war of the Holy People above the clouds, and now with the hissing of the Great Serpent in the deep, awful, and inaccessible valleys of the bright old inhabitants. [10] They overcame, he thought, the impediments of fire and storm; they charmed away the wrath of the evil spirits, and looked at length from the eastern ridge of those mighty hills upon the interminable glades and prairies spread out in their shade. Onward they went, he thought, till at length they saw rolling before them a mighty river, upon whose banks abode a nation of warriors, whose size was much greater than that of the Lenape, and who dwelt behind hills of their own making, whence they would make incursions into the territories of the neighbouring tribes. Before him stood one of the maidens of the land. She was beautiful as a straight tree, as a meadow of flowers, as a tree covered with blossoms, as a clear sky lit up with stars. Her voice was sweeter than the notes of the Mocking-Bird [11], and her eye brighter and softer than the eye of the mountain-goat. She wore a cloak made of the tender bark of the mulberry-tree, interlaced with the white feathers of the swan, and the gay plumage of the snake-bird, and the painted vulture. Strings of shells depended from her ancles, and flowers were braided into her hair. When she spoke to the young Lenape, it was with a soft voice, as if it would assure him, that the heart which dwelt within was as gentle as that voice, and as mild as that eye. He thought he wooed that maiden to be his wife, but, when she would have become such, and he would have pressed to his bosom the lovely flower of the giant people, there only appeared a little white dove which flew away, and nestled in the branches of the great medicine trees [12].

Then the dream of the warrior took another direction, and he had visions, and saw sights, and the phantoms of things more congenial to his disposition than even the smiles of beautiful maidens. He heard, in his sleep, the shrill war-cry of his nation, among whose foremost warriors he stood; and his ears were open to a loud shout of defiance from the enemy. He saw himself and his nation victorious, the Great River crossed, and the last canoe of his enemies committed in flight to its rapid bosom. The beautiful maiden became his wife. Again his course was onward like a torrent unchecked, and again other mountains opposed his course; but nothing offers insurmountable obstacles to the ardent spirit of an Indian warrior. He stands on the sunny brink of that mountain, and sees the beautiful lands spread out before his eye. A voice speaks to him from the hollow wind, "Warrior of the Lenni Lenape, how likest thou the land which I place before thee? The rivers are beautiful — are they not? and yet thou canst not see, as I see, their better part — the sleek and juicy fish which glide through them, or the fowls which feed on their margin. The forests are tall — are they not? but thine eyes do not pierce their glades as mine do, to behold the stately bucks which browze in their flowery copses, or the gay birds which sing their soft songs of love and joy, perched on the lofty branches of the chesnut and the hickory. I have given these lands to thy tribe, and thou shalt continue to occupy them till the coming of Miquon."

Wangewaha, or the Hard Heart, awoke from his dream, and calling together the priests and conjurors of the nation, related to them the strange things he had seen and heard in his sleep. The expounders of dreams gave it as their opinion, that the Great Spirit had bidden the familiar genius of the warrior to reveal to him the work to which he had ordained the Lenapes. They were unanimous in this opinion. Yet they advised, that the Master of Life should be consulted by sacrifices, after the due fasts should have been kept, and that his assistance should be supplicated by songs and dances(3), as they were ever wont to be. The advice of the expounders of dreams was followed, and the priests prepared for the fast. First they feasted themselves, and the chiefs, and warriors. The remains of the feast were then removed to the outside of the camp, and the crumbs carefully swept out, till the cabin, in which the fast was to be held, was as clean as the brow of a grassy hill after a summer rain. Then it was proclaimed aloud by the head priest, that the warriors and chiefs of the Lenape nation should enter the cabin, and observe the fast, and that the women and children, and all who are uninitiated in war, who had never hung up a scalp-lock in the temple of the Wahconda, nor offered a victim to the Great Star, should keep apart from those who had done both. When those who had bound themselves to observe the sacred ceremonial had entered the holy square appointed for the fast, a man armed with the weapons of war was stationed at each of the corners, to keep out every thing except the initiated. If a dog had but dared to breathe upon the sacred spot, he had met the fate of a thievish Flathead.

Then the Lenapes drank, as is their wont, of the root [13], which purges away their evil and cowardly inclinations and propensities, making them tellers of nothing but truth, bold and strong in war, cunning and dexterous in the theft of horses, patient in scarcity, and beneath the torments of the victor. The while they filled the air with loud invocations to the great Wahconda, and with petitions to him, that, in the succeeding sacrifice, he would reveal the meaning of the dream which had so filled their minds. Lest the unexpiated sins of the uninitiated, the women and the children, should stifle their own purer voices, the priest sent by the hands of the oldest of the women a portion of the small green leaves of the beloved weed [14] to the sinners. And thus, for three suns, the priests and warriors of the Lenapes ate no food, but mortified their sinful appetites to please the Master of Life.

The fast being over, and the expiation made, according to the customs of the nation, the multitude assembled to the feast and sacrifice. Proclamation was made, that, the holy rites being performed, it was lawful for the hungry to taste food. But first came the sacrifice.

The deer's flesh was laid on the burning coals, and the warriors who had fasted danced their most solemn dance around the hearth of sacrifice. The priest most reputed for intimacy with the Great Spirit, he who had oftenest, by his incantations, procured plentiful crops of maize, who had oftenest charmed the bisons to the unsheltered prairies, called the deer from the tangled coverts, and the horses from the hills of the Men of Black Garments [15], and given to the enemies of the Lenape the heart of the bird that runs low among the grass [16], arose, and began his hymn of supplication:

Song of the Lenape Priest.

Wangewaha dreamed a dream,
The Hard Heart slept,
When to him came the Manitou of Night,
And visions danced before his eyes.
What did Wangewaha see?
This he saw.

He saw the valiant warriors of his land,
Assembled as for warfare; wives and babes
Were at their feet; the aged on their sheds.
The dogs were harnessed;
The bones of many generations
Were taken from the burial places, where
They had reposed for countless suns;
The food was all prepared,
Dried corn and pemmican,
And folded tents proclaimed that the Lenapes
Had shod their mocassins for lengthened travel.

Dread Master of the earth,
Wahconda of the thunder, and the winds,
Who bid'st the earth shake, and the hills be thick
With hail and snow,
Shall we arise, and take
Our father's relics from the burial shed?
Shall we depart, and wilt thou guide
Our feet to fairer lands?

Does success await us,
In this, our distant pilgrimage?
Will these, our young men, strike and overcome?
Shall we possess the lands the dreamer saw?
And will their maidens look with favouring eyes
Upon our warriors?
Answer us, Spirit of the Mighty Voice!

Scarcely had the song of the priest ceased, when the voice of the Wahconda was heard sounding as sweetly as the notes of the mocking-bird rejoicing for the return of her mate, whom she chides for his long absence. The chiefs and warriors understood not the words he spoke, but they were heard by the priest, who repeated them to the awe-struck crowd. The Wahconda bade them gather up the bones of their fathers, burn them, and take the ashes, with which, and their women and children, and every thing they held valuable, they were to depart. They were to repair to the great Memahoppa, or Medicine Stone, which stood in the midst of a prairie, many suns beyond their hunting-grounds; and to this stone they were to be directed by a mighty wise man, of very low stature and of cross and passionate disposition, wearing a particoloured robe, and carrying a bag of rattles. Upon this memahoppa they would find further directions for their march engraved. Having pointed out their path, he gave them his blessing for brave men and expert horse-stealers, and his parting voice was as sweet as the voice of a maiden, who has died from ill-requited affection, and revisits the shades of earth in the form of a little white dove.

The Lenapes, having obeyed the orders of the Wahconda, set out on their march. The moment that their knapsacks were slung to their shoulders, and their journey made certain, the spirits of their departed friends struck up their glorious dance [17], far away over the great lakes, the favourite regions of the spirits of winds and tempests. The northern sky became lit all over with an effulgence brighter than that which glimmers in the Path of the Master of Life [18]. It was our departed friends who were showing their joy at the contemplated removal of our nation to the pleasant shades of the

Lenape wihittuck, and the rich and beautiful lands which fringe its border.

The Lenapes had not travelled very far, when they heard in the grass near them a loud shaking, which sounded like the rattling of nuts in a dry gourd, and soon they saw a little head with open jaws, and a tongue moving quicker than the sparkle of the fire-fly, peering out of the low grass. The Lenapes knew not what it was, but they saw that it assumed a menacing posture: so one went forward with his raised war-club to dispatch it. When he drew near, the unknown creature threw itself into the form which our white brother gives to his whip; the motion of his tail became so rapid, that it seemed but the soul of a vapour; his body swelled through excessive rage, till it became four times its former size, rising and falling like the Longknife's wind medicine [19]; his beautiful skin became speckled and rough, his head and neck flattened, his cheeks swollen with ungovernable anger, his lips drawn up, showing his dreadful fangs, his eyes red as burning coals, and his forked tongue of the colour of the hottest flame.

"Back, back," said he, "I am very passionate; I shall bite you. If you value your safety, go back before I make you very sorry that you have bit your thumb at me. Or, if you are really mad, let me know, that I may pity you, and not harm you."

Shamonekusse drew back with astonishment, and called the priest to come and talk with the strange creature. The priest, having made a short petition to his guardian Okki, which was the stuffed skin of a horned owl, came forward, and demanded of the strange creature, "Who are you?"

"I am," answered he, "the partisan leader of the rattlesnakes. I am the 'mighty wise man of very low stature, and of cross and passionate disposition, wearing a particoloured robe, and carrying a bag of rattles,' spoken of by the Great Wahconda, as he who was ordered to guide the Lenapes to the River of Fish."

"We are the Lenapes," answered the priest.

"Then you are the men I expected and was looking for," answered the chief of the rattlesnakes. "But why were you about to declare war against me — me, who alone possess, under the Wahconda, the means of conducting you in safety to the end of your journey? You are too brave and valiant, too hasty and choleric, Lenapes; it will be good for you to lose some of your blood to make you tamer."

"We are very sorry," answered the priest, perceiving the wisdom of conciliating the old fellow, "that the war-club was raised, and the hatchet raked up. It is our wish that the hatchet shall be buried again, and that there shall be a clear sky between us. Shall it be so, rattlesnake?"

"The hatchet shall be buried again, and there shall be a clear sky between us," answered the snake. "Yet, a little bird tells me that a black cloud shall arise, and that the hatchet may as well be put under the bedstead [20], whence it may be easily drawn forth. The rattlesnakes and the Lenapes, ere many suns shall pass, will be enemies, and each attempt the extermination of the other."

"Oh, we will not talk of that now," answered the priest; "we will put all thoughts of the evil day afar off. We will smoke with you, snake." So the Lenapes smoked with their new acquaintance; a firm league of peace was made between the two nations, and they became very good friends. They chatted for a long time of various matters, of the wars which the rattlesnakes had waged against the black snakes, the copperheads, the hornsnakes, and other warlike tribes of snakes. Again they moved on, the rattlesnake leading the way, till, much fatigued, their mocassins torn, and their wives cross, they spread their tents, and a night's encampment took place [21]. Again their course was onward, and again they encamped for another night. Spies were sent to search out the land, while the Lenapes travelled after at their leisure. At length the cunning old reptile, who still continued to guide them, declared that he saw, in the dry grass, foot-prints of men who were before them. While they halted, one went forward to reconnoitre. Soon he returned, and told our people that there was a band of Indians encamped in the path of the Lenapes, at a little distance from us. Our hot-blooded young warriors were for attacking them, but the wise old snake said, No. After offering many good reasons why peace should, at all times, be preferred to war, he advised, that a belt of wampum should be sent, and a league formed with them. The belt of wampum is delivered to a brave young warrior, Mottschujinga, or the Little Grizzly Bear.

This redoubted chief clothes himself in his best robe; he puts on his richest leggings; he fastens to his war-pipe the *trotters* of the fawn, and the cock-spurs of the wild turkey; he places in his scalp-lock the wing of the red-bird, the crest of the bittern, and the tail feathers of the pole-pecker. He paints one side of his face, to show that he can smoke in the war-pipe, which hangs in his belt, as gracefully and willingly as in the pipe of peace he carries in his hand, and as a fearless warrior, that his thoughts are quite as much of war as peace.

As he approaches the camp of the strange people, he puts on his most martial airs, and commences his song. He sings the lofty and warlike character of his nation, who never retreated from a foe, nor quailed before the stern glance of warriors; who can fast for seven suns, and, on the eighth, tire out the deer in his flight. He sings, that his fathers have been conquerors of all the tribes who roam between the mountains and the distant sea. He sings, that the maidens of his nation have eyes and feet like the antelope, that their songs are sweeter than the melodies of the song-sparrow, and their motions more graceful than the motions of a young willow, bowed by the wind. He sings, that the men of his tribe will smoke in the pipe of peace with the strange warriors, or they will throw a war-club into the council-house, as best suits them. The Lenapes are neither wom-en nor deer, they are not suing for peace, but they ask themselves why the great storm of war should arise, and the sky be overcast with the blustering clouds of tumult and quarrel. The Lenapes wish to go to the land of the rising sun; why should their path be shut up? their course is over a great river; why should it be made red with the blood of either nation? As he concluded his song, he held up the pipe of peace, the bowl of which was of red marble, the stem of which was of alder curiously carved, painted, and adorned with beautiful feathers. This, my brother must know is the symbol of peace among all the tribes of the wilderness.

A Brave, painted for war, met the messenger from the Lenape camp, and, after he had given his blanket to the winds, conducted him to the cabin of the assembled chiefs of his nation, not, however, before he had received the curses of the old women, and had been called "a wrinkled old man with a hairy chin and a flat nose."

Then meat was placed before the Lenape messenger. When he had satisfied his hunger, he pulled off his mocassins [22], and presented the pipe to the Brave who had been his conductor, who, filling it with tobacco and sweet herbs, handed it to him again. Then the youngest chief present took a coal from the fire, which flamed high in the centre of the council-cabin, and placed it on the beloved herb, which was made to smoke high. Mottschujinga then turned the stem of the pipe towards the field of the stars, to supplicate the aid of the Great Spirit, and then towards the bosom of his great mother, the earth, that the Evil Spirits might be appeased; now holding it horizontally, he moved round till he had made a circle, whereby he intimated that he sought to gain the protection of the spirits who sit on the clouds, and move in the winds of the air, of those who dwell in the deep and fearful glens and caverns, in the hollows of old and decayed oaks, on the summits of inaccessible hills, and within the limits of the great council-fire [23] of Michabou [24]. Having secured the aid of those invisible beings, in whose power it is to blow away the smoke of the pipe of peace, so that men shall speak from their lips only, and not from their hearts, and in consequence their promises shall be but as the song of a bird that has flown over, Mottschujinga presented his pipe to the great chief of the strangers, who, before he would smoke in it, arose and made a speech.

"Our tribe," said the chief, "are called Mengwe. We too have come from a distant country, and we also are bound to the land of the rising sun. We will smoke in the Lenape's pipe, and bury the war-club very deep; we will assist to make the Lenapes very strong, and will never suffer the grass to grow in our war-path when the Lenapes are assailed by enemies. We will draw out the thorns from your feet, oil your stiffened limbs, and wipe your bodies with soft down. We will lift each other up from this place, and the burthen shall be set down at each other's dwelling-place. And the peace we make shall last as long as the sun shall shine, or the rivers flow. And this is all I have to say."

So a league was made, though no war had been, and the two nations freely intermingled. Each man unclosed his hand to his neighbour, the Lenape warrior took the Mengwe maiden to his tent, and her brother had a woman of the former nation to roast his buffalo-hump, and boil his corn.

And now the spies, who had been sent forward for the purpose of reconnoitring, returned. They had seen many things so strange, that when they reported them, our people half-believed them to be dreams, and for a while regarded them but as the songs of birds. They told, that they had found the further bank of the River of Fish inhabited by a very powerful people, who dwelt in great villages, surrounded by high walls. They were very tall—so tall that the head of the tallest Lenape could not reach their arms, and their women were of higher stature and heavier limbs than the loftiest and largest man in the confederate nations. They were called the Allegewi, and were men delighting in red and black paint, and the shrill war-whoop, and the strife of the spear. Such was the relation made by the spies to their countrymen.

This report of the spies increased the fears and dissatisfaction of the Lenapes to such a height, that part agreed to remain in the lands in which they then were, and not to attempt to cross the river occupied by so many hostile warriors. But the greater part declared that they were men, and rather than turn back from a foe, however strong, or leave a battle-field without a blow or a war-whoop, they would march to certain death, and leave their bones in a hostile camp. So one band, the strongest of the Lenapes, remained beyond the Mississippi, while the others prepared to encounter the nations who were the present lords of the soil. But, ere they committed their fortunes to battle, they fasted, and mortified their flesh, to gain the favour of the being who presides over war, and their priests were consulted to learn whether he would be propitious to them. "Shall we conquer?" "Shall we overcome?" was eagerly asked. The priests replied, "The Lenapes shall overcome, when they have obtained the great war medicine." They asked what it was; the priests replied, "It shall be made known to you on the morrow." The morrow came, and the priests made known the great war medicine, whose properties brought certain victory to those possessed of it. In old times, the wild cat had devoured their people; they set a trap for him and caught him in it, burned his bones, and preserved the ashes. These ashes had been carefully kept by the priests, and they now brought them forth. The great old snake, the father of strife, was in the water; the old men gathered together and sang, and he shewed himself; they sang again, and he showed himself a little further out of the water; the third time he showed his horns. They were enabled to cut off one of the horns. He showed himself a fourth time, and they cut off the other horn. A piece of these horns, and the ashes of the bones of the wild cat compounded, was the great war medicine of our nation. Prepared with a medicine of such potency, the confederated nations moved towards the land of reported giants. When they had arrived on the banks of the Mississippi, they sent a message to the Allegewi, to request permission to settle themselves in their neighbourhood. That haughty people refused the request, but they gave them leave to pass through their country, and seek a settlement farther towards the land of the rising sun. The Lenapes accordingly began to cross the Mississippi, when the Allegewi, seeing that their bands were very numerous, outnumbering the birds on the trees or the fish in the waters, made a furious attack upon those who had crossed, threatening all with destruction, if they dared to persist in coming to their side of the river. Fired at the treachery of these people, and maddened with the loss of their brothers in arms, the Lenapes retired to the thick covert to consult on what was best to be done. It was deliberated in council, whether it was better to retreat in the best manner they could, or put forth their utmost strength, and let the enemy see they were not cowards, but men—brave men, who would not suffer themselves to be driven into the woods, before they had tested the strength of the enemy, and seen the power of their arms in hurling the spear, and striking with the war-club, and the truth of their eye in levelling the bow. It was determined, that brave men never turned back, that the Lenape were brave men, and must steep their mocassins in the blood of their enemies. The Mengwe, who till now had only looked on while our nation had done the fighting, offered to join our warriors, if, when the country was conquered, they should be allowed to share it with us. The proposal pleased our councillors, and the two nations renewed the faith of the calumet, resolved to conquer or die. The next sun was fixed on to attack the Allegewi in their intrenchments.

It was night; the bands of the confederate nations were sleeping in their cabins, dreaming dreams of victory and glory, when Wangewaha, or the Hard Heart, sleeping in his tent, was aroused by the tread of a light foot on the earth at his side, and the music of a voice sweeter than that of the linnet or the thrush. Looking up he saw, by the beams of the moon, a tall and beautiful woman, straight as a hickory, and graceful as a young antelope. She wore over her shoulders a cloak made of the tender bark of the mulberry, inter-laced with the white feathers of the swan, and the gay plumage of the snake bird and the painted vulture. Wangewaha started from his sleep, for he knew her to be the beautiful maiden whom he had seen in his dream, ere he quitted the land of his father's bones — the shape tall and erect, the eye black and sparkling, the foot small and swift, the teeth white and even, the glossy dark hair, and the small plump hand. He spoke to the beautiful stranger in mild accents, and the tones of her reply were as sweet as the breathings of a babe rocked to rest on the bough of a tree. He asked her who she was, and she replied she was a maiden from the camp of the Allegewi. "Why," he demanded, "had she come hither? Why had one so young and fair adventured her person in a hostile camp, in the dark hours of night, among fierce warriors, who had sworn the destruction of her nation?"

"I have come hither," replied the beautiful creature, "because I would escape the persecutions of a young warrior, the favourite of my father, who solicits me to become his wife. I love him not, I have told him so, yet he wishes to have me, while my heart revolts at the thought of becoming the companion of one, who boasts only the merit of being able to slay men weaker than himself; and of show-ing cheeks painted for war, and hands red with blood."

The Hard Heart, who felt not towards beautiful women the feel-ing which his name intimates, spoke to her words of consolation, and bade her go sleep with his sister, whom he called to him from another part of the cabin. But the passion of love arose in the warri-or's heart, and he determined that, if the Great Spirit should give him victory in the approaching contest, the beautiful maiden should become his wife.

The sun of the next morning shone on fields of slaughter and prodigies of valour. The confederated nations met the giant people; a great battle was fought, and many, very many, warriors fell. With the potent war-medicine of the Lenapes, borne by a priest, the confederates attacked their enemies, and were victors. The beaten and discomfited Allegewi retreated within the high banks which surrounded their villages and great towns, and there awaited the assault of our brave and fearless warriors. They were attacked, and numbers, greater than the forest leaves, fell in the first engagement. None were spared; the man who asked for quarter sooner received the arrow in his bosom — sooner felt the thrust of the spear, than he who was too brave to beg the poor boon of a few days longer stay on a cold and bleak earth, and preferred going hence without dishonour. Again, and again, were the Lenapes victorious. Beaten in many battles, and finding that complete extirpation awaited them, if they longer delayed flight, the Allegewi loaded their canoes with their wives and children, and took their course adown the broad bosom of the Mississippi. Never more were they or their descendants seen upon the lands where the Lenapes found them. Of all the countless throngs of the Allegewi, the beautiful maiden alone remained in our tents, and she was soon after taken to sleep in the bosom of Wangewaha.

"And now," said the chief of the rattlesnakes, "what do you propose to give me for my services? I have been a faithful and true guide, and have brought you safe through many dangers, to a land of plenty and glory. I deserve a recompense, surely."

"You do," answered the Hard Heart; "suppose we give you a pair of mocassins."

"Ha, ha! don't mention the thing again; it will throw me into a rage," answered the old fellow, beginning to flatten and swell at the joke. "But if you come to giving mocassins, they must be very many, for you know I have many legs. Suppose you give me a Lenape maiden to wife."

"Lenape maiden to wife! What will you do with a Lenape wife? Say, snake, what would be the cross between a rattlesnake and a Lenape?"

"Don't name the thing again, for I am very passionate," cried the old snake. "I shall bite. What would be the cross, say you? Why, the cleverest possible cross — the cross between a wise and valiant snake, and a beautiful woman, for a beautiful woman she will be, if I have the choosing of her. But, I demand as a recompense for my services, that I be allowed to unite myself in marriage with a woman of your nation. So set about it at once, for I am very hasty in these matters, and besides, wish to return to my nation, who have been for a long time without a leader."

Upon receiving this strange proposition, the Lenape chief to whom it was addressed called together the counsellors of the nation, and debated with them whether the request should be acceded to. Many were the arguments which were used for and against, but, at length, they came to the determination, that the wise old rattle-snake should have his choice of the Lenape maidens for a wife. The old fellow heard the acceptance of his proposal with much joy, for, as he said, he was of a very impatient temper, and in proportion as he bore crosses with a total want of patience, was his excessive joy, when he succeeded in his views and wishes. So the maidens were brought out, and he made choice of a beautiful girl, who had not seen the flowers bloom more than fifteen times. A tear trembled in the dark eye of this lovely maiden for a moment, at the thought of the strange and unequal match she was about to contract. But she was dazzled, as all women are, by the promised glory of becoming the bride of the great chief of a nation, and she wiped away the tears of regret, as women have often done before, with a leaf from the tree of consolation, and became joyous and light-hearted. They set off the next morning for the Valley of the Bright Old Inhabitants, and for greater speed she bore him on her shoulders, being the first bride that ever, as far as my knowledge goes, carried home her husband in a basket.

The confederates divided the lands they had conquered. The Mengwe took the lands which lay on the shores of the lakes of the north; the Lenapes chose those which received the beams of the warm suns of the south. Many, many ages passed away, the two nations continued at peace, the war-whoop was banished from the shades of either, and their numbers waxed very great. At length, some of our young hunters and warriors crossed the great glades [25], and travelled onward till they came to the beautiful Lenape wihittuck, where they have remained ever since. And this is the story which is told throughout the tribes of the wilderness, of the emigration of our people, and their victory over the original proprietors of the soil. I have done.

NOTES.

(1) *She became his without a wrestle.* — p. 143.

Hearne, in his Journey to the Frozen Ocean, says: — "It has ever been the custom, among those people, for the men to wrestle for any woman to whom they are attached; and, of course, the strongest party always carries off the prize. A weak man, unless he be a good hunter, and well beloved, is seldom permitted to keep a wife that a stronger man thinks worth his notice; for at any time when the wives of those strong wrestlers are heavily laden either with furs or provisions, they make no scruple of tearing any other man's wife from his bosom, and making her bear a part of his luggage. This custom prevails throughout all their tribes, and causes a great spirit of emulation among their youth, who are, upon all occasions, from their childhood, trying their strength and skill in wrestling ... The way in which they tear their women and children from one another, though it has the appearance of the greatest brutality, can scarcely be called fighting ... On these wrestling occasions the by-standers never attempt to interfere in the contest. It sometimes happens that one of the wrestlers is superior in strength to the other, and, if a woman be the cause of the contest, the weaker is frequently unwilling to yield, notwithstanding he is greatly overpowered. I observed that very few of those people were dissatisfied with the wives which had fallen to their lot, for, whenever any considerable number of them were in company, scarcely a day passed without some overtures being made for contests of this kind, and it was often very unpleasant to me to see the object of the contest sitting in pensive silence watching her fate, while her husband and his rival were contending for his prize. I have, indeed, not only felt pity for those poor wretched victims, but the utmost indignation, when I have seen them won, perhaps by a man whom they mortally hated. On these occasions, their grief and reluctance to follow their new lord has been so great, that the business has often ended in the greatest brutality; for, in the struggle, I have seen the poor girls stripped quite naked, and carried by main force to their new lodgings. At other times it was pleasant enough to see a fine girl led off the field from the husband she disliked, with a tear in one eye, and a finger in the other; for custom, or delicacy, if you please, has taught them to think it necessary to whimper a little, let the change be ever so much to their inclination."

(2) *Game of bones – gambling – games of chance.* – p. 143.

Gaming seems to be a natural passion of man, and is carried to a great excess among the American Indians. The games they play are various, but all are for the acquisition of coveted wealth; they never play without a stake, and that, considering the amount of their possessions, a very heavy one. They are emphatically gamblers. I have supposed that a description of their principal games may not be uninteresting to the reader, and have therefore subjoined the following: —

The game of the dish, which they call the *game of the little bones,* is only played by two persons. Each has six or eight little bones, which at first sight may be taken for apricot stones; they are of that shape and bigness. They make them jump up by striking the ground or the table with a round and hollow dish, which contains them, and which they twirl round first. When they have no dish, they throw the bones up in the air with their hands. If in falling they come all of one colour, he who plays wins five. The game is forty up, and they subtract the numbers gained by the adverse party. Five bones of the same colour win but one for the first time, but the second time they win the game. A less number wins nothing.

He that wins the game continues playing. The loser gives his place to another, who is named by the markers of his side; for they make parties at first, and often the whole village is concerned in the game. Oftentimes also, one village plays against another. Each party choses a marker, but he withdraws when he pleases, which never happens but when he loses. At every throw, especially if it happens to be decisive, they make great shouts. The players appear like people possessed, and the spectators are not more calm. They make a thousand contortions, talk to the bones, load the spirits of the adverse party with curses, and the whole village echoes with imprecations. If all this does not recover their luck, the losers may put off their party till next day. It costs them only a small treat from the company.

Then they prepare to return to the engagement. Each invokes his genius, and throws some tobacco in the fire to his honour. They ask him above all things for lucky dreams. As soon as day appears, they go again to play; but, if the losers fancy that the goods in their cabins made them unlucky, the first thing they do is to change them all. The great parties commonly last five or six days, and often continue all night. In the meantime, as all the persons present are in an agitation that deprives them of reason, they quarrel and fight, which never happens among the savages but on these occasions, and when they are drunk. One may judge, if, when they have done playing, they do not want rest.

It sometimes happens that these parties of play are made by order of the physician, or at the request of the sick. There needs no more for this purpose than a dream of one, or the other. This dream is always taken for the order of some spirit, and then they prepare themselves for play with a great deal of care. They assemble for several nights to try and to see who has the luckiest hand. They consult their genii, they fast, the married persons observe continence; and all to obtain a favourable dream. Every morning they relate what dreams they have had, and all things they have dreamt of, which they think lucky; and they make a collection of all, and put them into little bags, which they carry about with them; and, if any one has the reputation of being lucky, *that is*, in the opinion of these people, of having a familiar spirit more powerful, or more inclined to do good, they never fail to make him keep near him who holds the dish, they even go a great way to fetch him; and, if through age or any infirmity he cannot walk, they will carry him on their shoulders.

There is a game played by the Miamis, which is called the *game of straws*. These straws are small reeds, about the size of wheat straws, and about six inches long. They take a parcel, which are commonly two hundred and one, and always an odd number. After having shuffled them in well together, making a thousand contortions, and invoking the genii, they separate them with a kind of awl, or a pointed bone, into parcels of ten each: every one takes his own at a venture, and he that happens to get the parcel with eleven, gains a certain number of points that are agreed on. The whole game is sixty or eighty **** They have two games more, the first of which is called the *game of the bat*. They play at it with a ball, and sticks bent, and ending with a kind of racket. They set up two posts, which serve for bounds, and which are distant from each other according to the number of players. For instance, if they are eighty, there is half a league distance between the two posts. The players are divided into two bands, which have each their post. Their business is to strike the ball to the post of the adverse party without letting it fall to the ground, and without touching it with the hand; for, in either of these cases, they lose the game, unless he who makes the fault repairs it by striking the ball at one blow to the post, which is often impossible. These savages are so dexterous at catching the ball with their bats, that sometimes one game will last many days together.

The game described by Mackenzie, and called the *game of the platter*, is the same game, I think, that Charlevoix calls the "Game of the Bones." Of the passion for gaming of the Beaver Indians, see his Journal, 149. The same author (page 311), describes another game played by the Indians of the Rocky Mountains. It was played by two persons, each of whom had a "bundle of about fifty small sticks, neatly polished, of the size of a quill, and five inches long; a certain number of these sticks had red lines round them; and as many of these as one of the players might find convenient were curiously rolled up in dry grass, and, according to the judgment of his antagonist, respecting their number and marks, he lost or won."

(3) *Songs and Dances.* — p. 147.

Dancing is the favourite amusement of the savage, and one of his methods of propitiating the Deity. Does he feel cheerful, he dances; has he received benefits from a fellow-creature, he makes a dance to his honour; if from the Supreme Being, he gathers his tribe to his cabin, and gives thanks in a dance. When he has reason to fear his God is offended, or when an occurrence takes place, from which he draws an inference of his displeasure, he begins a solemn dance. Thus we have seen, that when the Dutch first landed on New York Island, the inhabitants, who believed them to be celestial beings, began a dance in order to propitiate them.

The dances of the savages are the common dance, and the dances which are held upon particular occasions, and the manner of dancing, varies somewhat. In dancing the *common dance*, they form a circle, and always have a leader, whom the whole company attend to. The men go before, and the women close the circle. The latter dance with great decency, as if engaged in the most serious business; they never speak a word to the men, much less joke with them, which would injure their character. They neither jump nor skip, but move lightly forward, and then backward, yet so as to advance gradually, till they reach a certain spot, and then retire in the same manner. They keep their bodies straight, and their arms hanging down close to their bodies. But the men shout, leap, and stamp, with such violence, that the ground trembles under their feet. Their extreme agility and lightness of foot is never displayed to more advantage than in dancing.

Of the dances held on particular occasions, there are many, and, unlike the last, these are frequent. "Of these," says Loskiel, "the chief is the *dance of peace*, called also the calumet or pipe dance, because the calumet or pipe of peace is handed about during the dance. This is the most pleasing to strangers who attend as spectators. The dancers join hands, and leap in a ring for some time. Suddenly the leader lets go the hand of one of his partners, keeping hold of the other. He then springs forward and turns round several times, by which he draws the whole company around, so as to be enclosed by them, when they stand close together. They disengage themselves as suddenly, yet keeping their hold of each other's hands during all the different revolutions and changes in the dance, which, as they explain it, represents the chain of friendship." This writer, who is in general very indifferent authority for what concerns the Indians, and must have made up his book from the relations of very careless or very stupid observers, never, I think from his own observation, differs very much in his account of this dance from Charlevoix, whose book generally is by far the best which has treated of the North American savages. He says, (vol. ii. p. 68) "They were young people equipped as when they prepare for the march; they had painted their faces with all sorts of colours, their heads were adorned with feathers, and they held some in their hands like fans. The calumet was also adorned with feathers, and was set up in the most conspicuous place. The band of music and the dancers were round about it, the spectators divided here and there in little companies, the women separate from the men. Before the door of the commandant's lodging, they had set up a post, on which, at the end of every dance, a warrior came up, and gave a stroke with his hatchet; at this signal there was a great silence, and this man repeated, with a loud voice, some of his great feats, and then received the applause of the spectators. When the dance of the calumet is intended, as it generally is, to conclude a peace, or a treaty of alliance against a common enemy, they grave a serpent on one side of the tube of the pipe, and set on one side of it a board, on which is represented two men of the two confederate nations, with the enemy under their feet, by the mark of his nation."

Of the two accounts which, it may be seen, differ essentially, I prefer Loskiel's. I think Charlevoix mistook another dance for the calumet dance, especially as he confesses they did him (the commandant) none of the honours which are mentioned. "I did not see the calumet presented to him, and there were no men holding the calumet in their hands."

The *war dance*, held either before or after a campaign, is their greatest dance. It is a dreadful spectacle, the object being to inspire terror in the spectators. No one takes a share in it, except the warriors themselves. They appear armed, as if going to battle. One carries his gun or hatchet, another a large knife, the third a tomahawk, the fourth a large club, or they all appear armed with tomahawks. These they brandish in the air, to signify how they intend to treat, or have treated, their enemies. They affect such an anger or fury on the occasion, that it makes a spectator shudder to behold them. A chief leads the dance, and sings the warlike deeds of himself or his ancestors. At the end of every celebrated feat of valour, he strikes his tomahawk with all his might against a post fixed in the ground. He is then followed by the rest, each finishing his round by a blow against the post. Then they dance all together, and this is the most frightful scene. They affect the most horrible and dreadful gestures, threatening to beat, cut, and stab each other. To complete the horror of the scene, they howl as dreadfully as in actual fight, so that they appear as raving madmen. Heckewelder's description agrees herewith. He remarks, that "Previous to going out on a warlike campaign, the war dance is always performed around the painted post. It is the Indian mode of recruiting. Whoever joins in the dance is considered as having enlisted for the campaign, and is obliged to go with the party."—*Heck. Hist. Acc.* p. 202. The description which Charlevoix gives of what he calls the "*dance of discovery*" among the

Iroquois, agrees so fully with the above account of the war dance, that we may presume it is the same, and that his is a new name for an old thing.

Charlevoix describes another dance, which he calls the *dance of fire*.

This last author describes another dance which is not mentioned by any other traveller; it is called, he says, the *dance of the bull*, and is thus described by him: "The dancers form several circles or rings, and the music, which is always the drum and the chickicoue, is in the midst of the place. They never separate those of the same family. They do not join hands, and every one carries on his head his arms and his buckler. All the circles do not turn the same way, and though they caper much, and very high, they always keep time and measure. From time to time, a chief of the family presents his shield: they all strike upon it, and at every stroke he repeats some of his exploits. Then he goes, and cuts a piece of tobacco at a post, where they have fastened a certain quantity, and gives it to one of his friends," &c. — *Charlevoix*, ii. 72.

The *dance of the green corn*, referred to in the text, or, more properly speaking, "the ceremony of thanksgiving for the first fruits of the earth," is described by Col. Johnston in vol. i. p. 286, of the Archælogia Americana. It does not differ materially from their common feasts. The principal ceremonies are described in the text.

The following is a description of the Powwah or black dance, by which the devil was supposed to be raised. "Lord's Day, September 1st. — I spent the day with the Indians on the island. As soon as they were up in the morning, I attempted to instruct them, and laboured to get them together, but quickly found they had something else to do; for they gathered together all their powwows, and set about a dozen of them to playing their tricks, and acting their frantic postures, in order to find out why they were so sickly, numbers of them being at that time disordered with a fever and bloody flux. In this they were engaged for several hours, making all the wild, distracted motions imaginable, sometimes singing, sometimes howling, sometimes extending their hands to the utmost stretch, spreading all their fingers, and seemed to push with them, as if they designed to fright something away, or at least keep it at arm's end; sometimes sitting flat on the earth, then bowing down their faces to the ground, wringing their sides, as if in pain and anguish, twisting their faces, turning up their eyes, grunting or puffing. These monstrous actions seemed to have something in them peculiarly fitted to raise the devil, if he could be raised by any thing odd and frightful. Some of them were much more fervent in the business than the others, and seemed to chant, peep, and mutter, with a great degree of warmth and vigour."—*Brainerd's Diary, E.*

GITTSHEE GAUZINEE.

Before the Bigknives or their fathers came to the land of the red men, the Indians generally, and the Chippewas in particular, were in the habit of burying many articles with the dead—if a warrior died, his weapons of war, his spear, his war-club, and his most valued trophies; if a hunter, his instruments of hunting were committed to the earth with him. His beaver-trap, his clothes, even a piece of roasted meat, and a piece of bread, were deposited with him in his grave. The scalps he had taken from the heads of his enemies, the skins of the bears slain by him in encounter foot to foot, were laid by his side, and, when the earth was thrown upon his breast, the utensils of less moment were laid upon his grave. If it was a woman who demanded the rites of burial, various articles which had been most useful to her in life were destined to the same service. As it was supposed that it would be her lot in the other world to perform, for the shades of her husband and family, the duties which she had performed for them while they were living in this, the various domestic implements used in the cabin were buried with her. This practice, once so universal, has been limited, since the coming of the white men among us, to comparatively a very few articles, such as the deceased was particularly fond of, or expressed a desire to have deposited with his or her body. The change I speak of was made in consequence of the following incident, which occurred in the life of a celebrated chief of former days, who had often led the Chippewas to victory and glory.

Gittshee Gauzinee, after an illness of only a few days, expired suddenly in the presence of his numerous friends, by whom he was greatly beloved, and deeply lamented. He had been an expert hunter, and had traversed the wild forests, and threaded the mazes of the wilderness, with a success rarely equalled. As a warrior there was none to surpass him: he could transfix two enemies with the same spear; his arm could bend a bow of twice the size of that bent by an ordinary arm; and his war-whoop sounded loud as the thunder of the moon of early corn. He was in the habit of cherishing, with deep and studious care, the weapons of war which had given him his glory, and among these he particularly attached great value to a fine gun which he had purchased of the first white man that had come to the city of the High Rock. It was with this gun that he had acquired his principal trophies, in remembrance of which he requested that it might be buried with him. But the importance attached to this article, which then was rarely met with among our people, and of great value, induced his friends to pause as to this injunction.

In the meantime, there were some who supposed that his death was not real, but that the functions of life were merely suspended, and would again be restored. On this account the body was not interred, but laid aside in a separate lodge, where it was carefully watched by his afflicted and weeping widow. It came to her mind that his spirit might not have left the tenement of clay; and she was inspired with fresh hopes of his restoration to life, when, upon laying her hand upon his breast above his heart, she could perceive a feeble pulsation. After the lapse of four days, their sanguine hopes were realised; he awoke, as if from a deep sleep, and complained of great thirst. By the kind attentions of his friends, and the use of certain drugs, with which every Indian is familiar, his health began to mend rapidly, and he was soon able to return to the hunt. When he was completely restored, he related the following account of his death, and recovery to life.

He felt, he said, cold chills creeping over him; his respiration became impeded; the dim and shapeless forms of things floated before his eyes, and sounds such as he had never heard before were ringing in his ears. He felt his breath come and go like the flashes of heat which dance before the wind on a summer's day. At length it went out to return no more, and he died.

After death he travelled on in the path of the dead for three days, without meeting with any thing extraordinary. He kept the road in which souls go to the Cheke Checkecame, and over mountains, and through valleys, pursued his way steadily. Hunger at length visited him, and he began to suffer much from want of food. When he came in sight of the village of the dead, he saw immense droves of stately deer, mooses, and other large and fat animals, browzing tamely near his path. This only served to aggravate his craving appetite, and excite more eagerly the feeling of hunger, because he had brought nothing with him wherewith to kill them. The animals themselves seemed sensible of his inability to do them harm, frolicking fearlessly around him, now bounding away over the plain in mimic terror, now advancing in gambols to his very feet. The deer skipped lightly along, while the moose followed with a more clumsy step; the wild cat suspended himself by his tail from the trees, while the bear rolled and tumbled on the green sod. Gittshee Gauzinee now bethought himself of the fine gun which he had left at home, and at once resolved to return and obtain it. On his way back, he met a great concourse of people, men, women, and children, travelling onward to the residence of the dead. But he observed that they were all very heavily laden with axes, kettles, guns, meat, and other things, and that each one as they passed uttered loud complaints of the grievous burdens with which the officious and mistaken kindness of their friends had loaded them. Among others, he met a man bowed down by age and infirmity, wearily journeying to the land of the dead, who stopped him to complain of the burthen his friends had imposed upon him, and this aged man concluded his address by offering him his gun, begging him to do so much towards relieving him of his load. Shortly after, he met a very old woman who offered him a kettle, and, a little further on, a young man who offered him an axe. He saw a beautiful and slender young maiden so heavily laden that she was compelled to rest her load against a tree, and a warrior bending under a weight twice as great as any that had ever yet been put on his shoulders. Gittshee Gauzinee accepted the various presents made him, out of courtesy and good nature, for he had determined to go back for his own gun, and other implements, and therefore stood little in need of these: so he journeyed back.

When he came near his own lodge, he could discover nothing but a long line of waving fire, which seemed completely to encircle it.

How to get across he could not devise, for, whenever he attempted to advance towards those places where the blaze seemed to be expiring, it would suddenly shoot up into brilliant cones, and pyramids of flame, and this was repeated as often as he approached it. At last he drew back a little, and made a desperate leap into the flames. The united effects of the heat, the violent exertion, and the fear of being burned in the desperate attempt, resulted in his restoration of life. He awoke from his trance, and, though weak and exhausted, he soon recovered his health and strength, and again made the valleys echo with his shouts of war and the hunt.

"I will tell you," said he to his friends, one night after his recovery, "of one practice in which our fathers have been wrong, very wrong. It has been their custom to bury too many things with the dead. Such burthens have been imposed upon them that their journey to the land of the dead has been made one of extreme labour and tediousness. They have complained to me of this, and I would now warn my brethren against a continuance of the practice. Not only is it painful to them, but it retards their progress in their journey. Therefore only put such things in the grave as will not be irksome to carry. The dress which the deceased was most fond of while living he should be clothed in when dead. His feathers, his head dress, and his other ornaments, are but light, and will be very agreeable to his spirit. His pipe also will afford him amusement on the road. If he has any thing more, let it be divided among his nearest relatives and friends, but on no account incumber his spirit with heavy and useless articles."

AMPATO SAPA.

Nothing, M. Verdier says, can be more picturesque and beautiful than the cascade of St. Anthony, so renowned in the topography of the western world. The irregular outline of the Fall, by dividing its breadth, gives it a more impressive character, and enables the eye more easily to take in its beauties. An island, stretching in the river both above and below the Fall, separates it into two unequal parts. From the nature of the rock which breaks into angular, and apparently rhomboidal fragments of a huge size, this fall is subdivided into small cascades, which adhere to each other, so as to form a sheet of water, unrent, but composed of an alternation of retiring and salient angles, and presenting a great variety of shapes and shades. Each of these forms is in itself a perfect cascade. When taken in one comprehensive view they assume a beauty of which we could scarcely have deemed them susceptible. Few falls assume a wilder and more picturesque aspect than these. The thick growth of oaks, hickory, walnut, &c. upon the island, imparts to it a gloomy and sombre aspect, contrasting pleasingly with the bright surface of the watery sheet which reflects the sun in many differently coloured hues. All travellers have spoken of it as possessing wonderful beauties, and the poor unenlightened Indian, who ascribes every thing of an imposing, a sublime, and a magnificent character, every thing which has phenomena he cannot comprehend to a superior being, and who fancies a governing spirit in every deep glen in the wilderness, has associated many of his wild and fanciful traditions with this singular spot. The following favourite tale of, the Dahcotah is not the only tradition connected with this romantic spot.

An Indian of the Dahcotah nation had united himself early in life to a youthful female, whose name was Ampato Sapa, which signifies, in the Dahcotah language, the *Dark-day*. With her he lived for many years very happily; their days glided on like a clear stream in the summer noon. There were few husbands and wives who enjoyed as much nuptial happiness as fell to the lot of this Indian couple. Among that people the duties allotted to the female sex are both laborious and incessant; with Ampato Sapa, they were ameliorated by the kindness of her husband, who, in defiance of the customs of our people, performed the greater part of her tasks herself. Their union had been blessed with two children, upon whom both parents doated with a depth of feeling unknown to those who have other treasures besides those which spring from nature. The man had acquired a reputation as a hunter, which drew around him many families who were happy to place themselves under his protection, and avail themselves of such part of his chace, as he needed not for the support of his family. Desirous of strengthening their interest with him, some of them invited him to form a connexion with their family, observing, at the same time, that a man of his talents, and present and increasing importance, required more than one woman, to wait upon the numerous guests whom his reputation would induce to visit his lodge. They assured him that he would soon be acknowledged as a chief, and that in this case a second wife was indispensable. Their pleadings and flattery infused new ideas into his mind, and ambition soon succeeded in dispelling love, and the remembrance of years of conjugal endearment. Fired with the thought of obtaining high honours, he resolved to increase his importance by a union with the daughter of an influential man of his tribe. He had accordingly taken a second wife, without having ever mentioned the subject to his former companion, being desirous to introduce his bride into his lodge, in the manner which should be least offensive to the mother of his children, for whom he yet retained much regard, though bad ambition "had induced him to countenance a divided bed and affections." It became necessary, however, that he should break the matter to her, which he did as follows: "You know," said he, "that I can love no woman so fondly as I doat upon you. You were the first woman I loved, and you are the only one. With regret have I seen you of late subjected to toils which must be oppressive to you, and from which I would gladly relieve you, yet I know of no other way of doing so, than by associating to you, in the household duties, one who shall relieve you from the trouble of entertaining the numerous guests whom my growing importance in the nation collects around me. I have, therefore, resolved to take another wife, but she shall always be subject to your controul, as she will always rank in my affections second to you."

With the utmost anxiety and deepest concern did his companion listen to this unexpected proposal. She expostulated in the kindest terms; entreated him with all the arguments which undisguised love and the purest conjugal affection could suggest. She replied to all the objections he had raised, and endeavoured to dispel all the clouds his seemingly disinterested kindness had thrown over her present situation. Desirous of winning her from her opposition, he concealed the secret of his union with another, while she redoubled her care and exertion, to convince him that she was equal to all the tasks imposed upon her by his increasing reputation and notoriety. When he again spoke on the subject, she pleaded all the endearments of their past life; she spoke of his former kindness for her, of his regard for her happiness, and that of their mutual offspring; she bade him beware of the fatal consequences of this purpose of his.

Finding her bent upon withholding her consent to his plan, he informed her that all opposition on her part was unavailing, as he had already selected another partner; and that, if she could not see his new wife as a friend, she must receive her as a necessary incumbrance, for he was resolved that she should be an inmate in his house. The poor Dark-Day heard these words in silent consternation. Watching her opportunity, she stole away from the cabin with her infants, and fled to her father, who lived at a considerable distance from the place of her husband's residence. With him she remained until a party of Dahcotahs went up the Mississippi, on a winter's hunt. Not caring whither she went, so it was not to the lodge of her faithless husband, she accompanied them. All hope had left her bosom, and even her interest in her children had faded with the decay of the impassioned love she had felt for their father. The world, the simple pleasures of Indian life, had no farther charm for Ampato Sapa. She would wander for hours, listless and tearful, by the shaded river bank, or gaze in the night with a distracted look upon the silver moon and star-lit sky. At times, as if fearful of impending pursuit, she would snatch up her children, and rush out into the woods. The Red Man of the forest has a kind of instinctive veneration for madness(1) in every form; the mere supposition of such a misfortune has procured the liberation of a victim bound to the stake, whom no arts or persuasion could operate to save. The people of her tribe saw, with deep commiseration, the seeming aberration of intellect of the poor Indian woman, but, knowing little of the feeling which possessed her bosom, could apply no healing medicine.

In the spring, as they were returning with their canoes loaded with furs, they encamped near the falls which our white brother has seen, and which have became so celebrated in Indian story for the many tragical scenes connected with them. In the morning, as they left their encamping ground on the border of the river, she for a while lingered near the spot, as if working up her mind to some terrible feat of despair. Then, launching her light canoe, she entered it with her children, and paddled down the stream, singing her death-song. The air was one of those melancholy airs which are sung by our people when in deep distress, or about to end the journey of life.

Death-Song of Ampato Sapa.

I loved him long and well.
And he to me
Was the soft sun, which makes the young trees bud.
In gentle spring,
And bids the glad birds sing,
From out the boughs, their song of love and joy.
And he would sit beside me on the grass,
And plait my hair with beads,
And tell the trees, and flowers, and birds,
That Dark-Day was more beautiful than they.

I lov'd him long and well.
And he to me
Was as the tree which props the tender vine,
Or clustering ivy, letting them embrace
His strength and pride.
When he withdraws from them,
They fall, and I must die.

He lov'd me once,
And lov'd his little babes;
And he would go with morning to the hills,
And chase the buffalo.

But he would come
And press me in his arms, when darkness hid
Both beast and bird from the clear hunter's eye.
Then he would creep to where our children slept,
And smile—but sweeter smile upon their mother.

He loves another now.
A younger bird is in his nest,
And sings sweet songs from Dark-Days once fair bower,
And I am lov'd no more.
He will be no more to me as the sun,
Which gives the young trees life in gentle spring.
Nor as the tree which props the tender vine.

He loves another better than Dark-Day —
He cares not for her,
Nor for his children:
No, he cares not for them.

I will die;
I will go to the happy lands,
Beyond the mighty river.
There I shall see again my tender mother,
There I shall meet the warriors of my tribe,
And they shall make my sons good men.
There I shall meet, ere many moons be past,
My husband reconcil'd to me, and he
Again shall sit beside me on the grass,
And plait my hair with beads,
And tell the trees, and birds, and flowers,
That Dark-Day is more beautiful than they.

As she paddled her canoe down the stream, her friends perceived her intent, but too late; their persuasions and attempts to prevent her from proceeding were of no avail. She continued to sing, in a mournful voice, the past pleasures which she had enjoyed while she was the undivided object of her husband's affections: at length, her voice was drowned in the sound of the cataract; the current carried down her frail bark with inconceivable rapidity; it came to the edge of the precipice, was seen for a moment enveloped with spray, but never after was a trace of the canoe or its passengers discovered. Yet the Indians imagine that often in the morning a voice is heard singing a mournful song along the edge of the fall, and that it dwells on the inconstancy of a husband. They assert that sometimes a white dove is seen hovering over the neighbouring sprays; at other times, Ampato Sapa wanders in her proper person near the spot, with her children wrapped in skins, and pressed to her bosom.

NOTE.

(1) *Instinctive veneration for madness.* — p. 194.

Insanity is not common among the Indians. Men in this unhappy situation are always considered as objects of pity. Every one, young and old, feels compassion for their misfortune; to laugh or scoff at them would be considered as a crime, much more so to insult or molest them. Heckewelder tells the following story concerning their treatment of one suspected of insanity, which proves their peculiar feeling with regard to this unfortunate class of men: —

"About the commencement of the Indian war of 1763, a trading Jew, who was going up the Detroit river with a bateau load of goods which he had brought from Albany, was taken by some Indians of the Chippewas nation, and destined to be put to death. A Frenchman, impelled by motives of friendship and humanity, found means to steal the prisoner, and kept him so concealed for some time, that, although the most diligent search was made, the place of his confinement could not discovered. At last, however, the unfortunate man was betrayed by some false friend, and again fell into the power of the Indians, who took him across the river to be burned and tortured. Tied to the stake, and the fire burning by his side, his thirst from the great heat became intolerable, and he begged that some drink might be given him. It is a custom with the Indians, previous, to a prisoner being put to death, to give him what they call his last meal; a bowl of pottage or broth was therefore brought to him for that purpose. Eager to quench his thirst, he put the bowl immediately to his lips, and, the liquor being very hot, he was dreadfully scalded. Being a man of a very quick temper, the moment he felt his mouth burned, he threw the bowl with its contents full into the face of the man who had handed it to him. 'He is mad! he is mad!' resounded from all quarters. The by-standers considered his conduct as an act of insanity, and immediately untied the cords with which he was bound, and let him go where he pleased."

THE CAVERNS OF THE KICKAPOO.

The scenery of the Prairie *des Chiens* is among the most beautiful of the western wilderness—nothing presents finer views than may be had from the lofty hills, which lie east of the Wisconsan. The prairie extends about ten miles along the eastern bank of the river, and is limited on that side by the before-mentioned hills, which rise to the height of about four hundred feet, and run parallel with the course of the river, at a distance of about a mile and a half from it. On the western bank, the bluffs which rise to the same elevation are washed at their base by the river. From the top of this majestic hill, which is called Pike's Mountain, there is a beautiful and magnificent view of the two rivers, Wisconsan and Mississippi, which mingle their waters at its foot. The prairie has retained its old French appellation, derived from an Indian who formerly resided there, and was called the Dog. The hill, or Pike's Mountain, has no particular limits in regard to extension, being merely a part of the river bluffs, which stretch along the margin of the river on the west for several miles, and retain nearly the same elevation above the water. The side fronting upon the river is so abrupt as to render the summit completely inaccessible even to a pedestrian, except in a very few places, where he may ascend by taking hold of the bushes and rocks that cover the slope. In general the acclivity is made up of precipices arranged one above another, some of which are a hundred and fifty feet high.

In one of the niches or recesses formed by one of these precipices, in the cavern of Kickapoo creek, which is a tributary of the Wisconsan, there is a gigantic mass of stone presenting the appearance of a human figure. It is so sheltered by the overhanging rocks, and by the sides of the recess in which it stands, as to assume a dark and gloomy character.

Has my brother—said the Indian chief to the traveller—ever heard how a beautiful woman of my nation became an image of stone? If he has, let him say so; if he has not, the Guard of the Red Arrows will tell him the story.

Once upon a time, many, very many ages ago, there lived in my nation a woman who was called Shenanska, or the White Buffalo Robe. She was an inhabitant of the prairie, a dweller in the cabins which stand upon the verge of the hills. She was the pride of our nation, not so much for her beauty, though she was exceedingly beautiful, as for her goodness, which made her beloved of all. The breath of the summer wind was not milder than the temper of Shenanska, the face of the sun was not fairer than her face. There was never a gust in the one, never a cloud passed over the other. Who but Shenanska dressed the wounds of the Brave when he returned from battle? who but she interceded for the warrior who came back from the fight without a blow? yet who was it encouraged him to wipe the black paint from the memory of his tribe by brave deeds? It was she who dreamed the dreams that led to the slaughter of the Sauks and the Foxes; it was she who pointed out the favourite haunts of the deer and the bison. When the warriors returned victorious from the field of blood, it was she who came out with songs sweeter than the music of the dove; and, when they brought no scalps, it was she who comforted them with stories of past victories, and dreams of those which were yet to be. Before she had seen the flowers bloom twice ten times, she had been by turns the wife of many warriors, for all loved her.

At length, it became the fortune of our tribe to be surprised in our encampment on the banks of the Kickapoo, by a numerous band of the bloody and warlike Mengwe. Many of our nation fell fighting bravely, the greater part of the women and children were scalped, and the remainder were compelled to fly to the wilds for safety. It was the fortune of Shenanska to escape from death, and perhaps worse evils. When the alarm of the war-whoop reached her ear, as she was sleeping in her lodge in the arms of her husband; she arose, and seizing her lance, and bow and arrows, she rushed with the Braves to battle. When she saw half of the men of her nation lying dead around, then she fled, and not till then. Though badly wounded, she succeeded in effecting her escape to the hills. Weakened by loss of blood, she had not strength enough left to hunt for a supply of food; she was near perishing with hunger.

Designed & Etched by W. H. Brooks, A. R. E. A.
The Spirit breathed on her & she became Stone. *page 104.*
London, Published by Colburn & Bentley, April 1830

While she lay in this languishing state beneath the shade of a tree, there came to her a Being, who was not of this world. He said to her, in a gentle and soothing voice, "Shenanska! thou art wounded and hungry, shall I heal thee and feed thee? Wilt thou return to the lands of thy tribe, and live to be old, a widow and alone, or go now to the land of departed spirits, and join the shade of thy husband? The choice is thine. If thou wilt live crippled, and bowed down by wounds and disease, thou mayest; if thou better likest to rejoin thy friends in the country beyond the Great River, say so." Shenanska replied, that she wished to die. The Spirit then took her in his arms, and placed her in one of the recesses of the cavern, overshadowed by hanging rocks. He then spoke some low words, and, breathing on her, she became stone. Determined that a woman so good and so beautiful should not be forgotten by the world, nor be deprived of the ability of protecting herself from mutilation, he imparted to her statue the power of killing suddenly any Indian that approached near it. For a long time the statue relentlessly exercised this power. Many an unconscious Indian, venturing too near, fell dead without wound or bruise. At length, tired of the havoc it had made, the guardian Spirit took away the power he had given. At this day the

116

statue may be approached with safety. Yet the Indian people hold it in fear and veneration, and none passes it without paying it the homage of a sacrifice. This is my story.

THE MOUNTAIN OF LITTLE SPIRITS.

At the distance of a woman's walk of a day from the mouth of the river called by the pale-faces the Whitestone, in the country of the Sioux, in the middle of a large plain, stands a lofty hill or mound. Its wonderful roundness, together with the circumstance of its standing apart from all other hills, like a fir-tree in the midst of a wide prairie, or a man whose friends and kindred have all descended to the dust, has made it known to all the tribes of the West. Whether it was created by the Great Spirit, or piled up by the sons of men, whether it was done in the morning of the world, or when it had grown fat and stately, ask not me, for I cannot tell you. Those things are known to one, and to one only. I know it is called by all the tribes of the land the Hill of Little People, or the Mountain of Little Spirits. And the tradition is yet freshly traced out on the green leaf of my memory, which has made it the terror of all the surrounding nations, and which fills the Sioux, the Mahas, the Ottoes, and all the neighbouring tribes, with great fear and trembling, whenever their incautious feet have approached the sacred spot, or their avocation compels them to look at the work of spirits. No gift can induce an Indian to visit it, for why should he incur the anger of the Little People who dwell within it, and, sacrificed upon the fire of their wrath, behold his wife and children no more? In all the marches and countermarches of the Indians; in all their goings and returnings; in all their wanderings, by day and by night, to and from lands which lie beyond it; their paths are so ordered that none approach near enough to disturb the tiny inhabitants of the hill. The memory of the red man of the forest has preserved but one instance where their privacy was violated, since it was known through the tribes that they wished for no intercourse with mortals. Before that time many Indians were missing every year. No one knew what became of them, but they were gone, and left no trace nor story behind. Valiant warriors filled their baskets with dried corn, and their quivers with tough arrow shafts and sharp points; put new strings to their bows; new shod their mocassins, and sallied out to acquire glory in

combat: but there was no wailing in the camp of our foes; their arrows were not felt, their shouts were not heard. Yet they fell not by
the hands of their foes; but perished, we know not where or how. At
length, the sun shone on the mystery, and the parted clouds displayed a clear spot. Listen!

Many seasons ago, there lived within the limits of the great council-fire of the Mahas, a chief who was renowned for his valour and
victories in the field, his wisdom in the council, his dexterity and
success in the chase. His name was Mahtoree, or the White Crane.
He was celebrated throughout the vast regions of the west, from the
Mississippi to the Hills of the Serpent [26], from the Missouri to the
Plains of Bitter Frost, for all those qualities which render an Indian
warrior famous and feared. He was the terror of his enemies, whom
in the conflict he never spared; the delight as well as refuge of his
friends, whom he never deserted. Yet, brave as he was, and fierce
and reckless when met in the strife of warriors, never did his valour,
or his fierceness, or his recklessness of danger, betray him into those
excesses of wrath and cruelty, which, after great victories purchased
by much blood and loss of dear and valued friends, will often be
seen in the camp of the red man of the forest. Never by his counsels
was the captive tortured—never by his command were weak and
defenceless women and children delivered over to slaughter. He
had frequently been known, at the voice of pity crying at the door of
the heart, and at the suggestions of a great and proud mind, to cut
the bonds which bound the victim to the stake, thereby exposing
himself to the wrath and anger of his stern warriors, and to rage
which, but for the unequalled valour and daring boldness and wisdom of his career, both as a warrior and a man, would have been
attended with death to himself, and the entailment of infamy upon
his name. It has already been told our brother, that none but a noted
and approved warrior dare take upon himself the liberation of a
prisoner, devoted by the spirit of Indian warfare to tortures and
death.

In one of the war expeditions of the Pawnee Mahas against the
Burntwood Tetons, it was the good fortune of the former to overcome, and to take many prisoners—men, women, and children. One
of the captives, Sakeajah, or the Bird-Girl, a beautiful creature in the
morning of life, after being adopted into one of the Mahas families,

became the favourite wife of the chief warrior of the nation. Great was the love and affection which the White Crane bore his beautiful wife, and it grew yet stronger in his soul, when she had brought him four sons—a gift the more highly prized by the wise and sagacious chief, because, as my brother can see, for he is not a fool, it was the pledge of continued power and importance in the tribe, when his own strength and vigour should have passed away, when the hand of age should no more find joy in bending the bow, and the trembling knee be best pleased to rest upon soft skins by the warm fire of the cabin. Among the children of the forest he is most valued who has provided most plentifully the means to maintain the honour, and secure the safety, of his people; and hence he who can reckon the most brave and warlike sons is esteemed the greatest of benefactors. Among all the red men of the land, that wife acquires the strongest hold on the affections of her husband who has given him the largest family, as that husband acquires the greatest consequence in the eyes of his nation, who sees the most birds in his nest, and is able to carry most vultures to prey upon the corpses of his enemies. Is the barren woman beloved by her husband? Ask me if the male bird watches by the nest of her who sits on addled eggs. I shall tell you "No," nor does the husband love or value the wife who lives alone in his cabin with none to call her mother.

The beautiful Sakeajah gave her husband but one daughter, and upon her did her parents lavish all those affections which had not their origin in war and bloodshed. The sons were loved for the promise they gave of bending their father's bow, and raising his massy club in battle, and shouting his terrible war-cry with the ability to make good the threats it contained—with the daughter were linked the few pacific remembrances which find entrance into that stony thing—an Indian's heart. And well was Tatoka, or the Antelope, for that was the name of the daughter of Mahtoree and Sakeajah, worthy to be loved. She was beautiful, as young Indian maidens generally are, before the hard duties of the field and the cabin have bowed their limbs, and servitude has chilled the fire of their hearts. Her skin was but little darker than that of the chief from the far land who is listening to my story. Her eyes were large and bright as those of the bison-ox, and her hair black and braided with beads, brushed, as she walked, the dew from the flowers upon the prairies. Her temper was soft and placable, and her voice—what is so sweet as the voice of an Indian maiden when tuned to gladness! what so moves the hearer to grief and melancholy by its tones of sorrow and anguish! Our brother has heard them—let him say if the birds of his own forests, the dove of his nest, have sweeter notes than those he hears warbled in the cabin of the red man. His eyes say no. It is well.

It may not be doubted that the beautiful Tatoka had many lovers; there was not a youth in the nation, whose character authorised the application, that did not become a suitor to the fair daughter of the White Crane. But the heart of the maiden was touched by none of them; she bade them all depart as they came; she rejected them all. The father who loved his daughter too well to sell her as he would a beaver-trap or a moose-skin, or to compel her to become a wife, would have been glad to see her choose a protector from among the many Braves who solicited her affections. But, with the perverseness which is often seen among women, who are but fools at best, though made to be loved, she had placed her affections upon a youth, who had distinguished himself by no valiant deeds in war, nor even by industry or dexterity in the chase. His name had never reached the surrounding nations; his own nation knew him not, unless it was as a weak and imbecile man: he was poor in every thing that constitutes the riches of Indian life, and poorer still in spirit and acquirements. Who had heard the twanging of Karkapaha's bow in the retreats of the bear? or who beheld the war-paint on his cheek or brow?—Where were the scalps or the prisoners that betokened his valour or daring? No song of valiant exploits had been heard from his lips, for he had none to boast of—if he had done aught becoming a man, he had done it when none were by. The beautiful Tatoka, who knew and lamented the deficiencies of her lover, strove long to conquer her passion; but, finding the undertaking beyond her strength, surrendered herself to the sweets of unrepressed affection, and urged her heart no more to the unequal task of subduing her love. Their stolen interviews were managed with much care, and for a long time no one suspected them; but at length the secret of their love and the story of their shame became so apparent as to do away the possibility of further concealment. The lovers were in an agony of fear and terror. Though beloved by her father, she had no reason to hope that he would so far forget his dignity and the honour of his family, and so far sacrifice his views of aggrandizement, as to admit into his family a man who was neither hunter nor warrior, and whose want of qualifications would have ensured his rejection by families of ordinary note—how much more from that of a proud and haughty chief! Love conquers the strongest; and, rather than be separated, those who love each other well will dare every danger. Rather than be torn apart, the fond pair, whose affections were strengthened by the pledge of love which Tatoka bore about her, determined to fly the anger of the father. The preparations for flight were made, the night fixed upon came, and they left the village of the Mahas and the lodge of Mahtoree for the wilderness.

With all their precautions, and supposed exemption from suspicion, their flight was not unmarked: their intimacy had been for some time suspected; but it was only the day preceding their elopement that the mother had discovered undoubted proofs of their guilty intimacy. When the justly indignant father was made acquainted with the disgrace which had befallen his house, he called his young men around him, and bade them pursue the fugitives, promising his daughter to whomsoever should slay the ravisher. Immediate pursuit was made, and soon a hundred eager youths were on the track of the hapless pair. With that unerring skill and sagacity in discovering foot-prints which mark our race, their steps were tracked, and themselves soon discovered retreating. But what was the surprise and consternation of the pursuers, when they found that the path taken by the hapless pair would carry them to the Mountain of Little Spirits, and that they were sufficiently in advance to reach it before the pursuers could come up with them! None durst venture within the supposed limits, and they halted till the White Crane should be informed of their having put themselves under the protection of the spirits.

In the mean time the lovers pursued their journey towards the fearful residence of the little people of the hill. Despair lent them courage to do an act to which the stoutest Indian resolution had hitherto been inadequate. They determined, as a last resource, to tell their story to the spirits, and demand their protection. They were within a few feet of the hill, when, in a breath, its brow, upon which

no object till now had been visible, became covered with little people, the tallest of whom was not higher than the knee of the maiden,
and many of them, but these children, were of lower stature than
the squirrel. Their voice was sharp and quick, like the barking of the
prairie dog; a little wing came out at each shoulder; each had a single eye, which eye was a right in the men, and in the women a left;
and their feet stood out at each side. They were armed as Indians
are armed, with tomahawks, spears, and bows and arrows. He who
appeared to be the head chief, for he wore the air of command and
the eagle feather of a leader, came up to them, and spoke as follows: —

"Why have you invaded the village of a race whose wrath has
been so fatal to your people? How dare you venture within the
sacred limits of our residence? Know you not that your lives are
forfeited?"

The trembling pair fell on their knees before the little people, and
Tatoka, for her lover had less than the heart of a doe, and was
speechless, related her story. She told them how long she had loved
Karkapaha, and holding down her head confessed her fatal indis-
cretion. Then she pictured the wrath of her father, the pursuit which
was making, doubtless with a view to the punishment by death of
her lover, and concluded her tale of sorrow with a burst of tears,
which came from her eyes like the rain from a summer cloud, and
sighs which might be compared to summer winds breathing from a
bed of flowers. The little man who wore the eagle's feather appeared very much moved with the sorrows of the pair, and calling
around him a large number of men, who were doubtless the chiefs
and counsellors of the nation, a long consultation took place. The
result was a determination to favour and protect the lovers. They
had but just talked themselves into a resolution to inflict vengeance
on all who should approach the hill with the intent to injure the pair
who had thrown themselves upon their protection, when Shongotongo, or the Big Horse, one of the Braves whom Mahtoree had
dispatched in quest of his daughter, appeared in view in pursuit of
the fugitives. It was not till Mahtoree had taxed his courage that the
Big Horse had ventured on the perilous and fearful quest. He approached with the strength of heart and singleness of purpose
which accompany an Indian warrior who deems the eyes of his

nation upon him. When first the Brave was discovered thus wantonly, and with no other purpose but the shedding of blood, intruding on the dominions of the spirits, no words can tell the rage which appeared to possess their bosoms, manifesting itself in a thousand wild and singular freaks of passion and coarseness of language. Secure in the knowledge of their power to repel the attacks of every living thing, the intrepid Maha was permitted to advance within a few steps of Karkapaha. He had just raised his spear to strike the unmanly lover, when, all at once, he found himself riveted to the ground: his feet refused to move; his hands, which he attempted to raise, hung powerless at his side; his tongue, when he attempted to speak, refused to utter a word. The bow and arrow fell from his hand, and his spear lay powerless. A little child, not so high as the fourth leaf of the thistle, came and spat upon him, and a company of young maidens, whose feet were not longer than the blue feather upon the wing of the teal, danced a mirthsome dance around him, singing a taunting song of which he was the burthen. All and each of the tiny spirits did their part towards inflicting pain and ignominy on the hapless Maha. When they had finished their task of punishing by preparatory torture, a thousand little Spirits drew their bows, and a thousand winged arrows pierced his heart. In a moment, a thousand mattocks, of the size of an Indian's thumb-nail, were employed in preparing him a grave. And he was hidden from the eyes of the living, ere Tatoka could have thrice counted over the fingers of her hand.

When this was done, the chief of the Little Spirits called Karkapaha to his seat, and spoke to him thus: — "Maha, you have the heart of a doe; you would fly from a roused wren. Cowards find no favour in the eyes of the spirits of the air, who do not know what fear is, save when they see it painted on the cheeks of a mortal. We have not spared you because you deserved to be spared, but because the maiden loves you, and we would pleasure her. It is for this purpose that we will give you the heart of a man, that you may return to the village of the Mahas, and find favour in the eyes of Mahtoree and the Braves of the nation. We will take away your cowardly spirit, and will give you the spirit of the warrior whom we slew, whose heart was firm as a rock, and whose knees would have trembled when mountains caught the touch of fear, and not before. Sleep, man of little soul, and wake to be better worthy the love of the beauteous Antelope."

Then a deep sleep came over the Maha lover. How long he slept he knew not, but when he woke he felt at once that a change had taken place in his feelings and temper. The first thought that came to his mind was a bow and arrow; the second the beautiful Indian girl who lay sleeping at his side. The Little Spirits had disappeared—not a solitary being, of the many thousands, who, but a few minutes before, peopled the hill and filled the air with their discordant cries, was now to be seen or heard. At the feet of Karkapaha lay a tremendous bow, larger than any bowman ever yet used, and a sheaf of arrows of proportionate size, and a spear of a weight which no Maha could wield. Wonder of wonders! the weak and slender Karkapaha could draw that bow, as an Indian boy bends a willow twig, and the spear seemed in his hand but a reed, or a feather. The shrill war-whoop burst unconsciously from his lips, and his nostrils seemed dilated with the fire and impatience of a newly-awakened courage. The heart of the fond Indian girl dissolved in tears, when she saw these proofs of strength and those evidences of spirit, which, she knew, if they were coupled with valour—and how could she doubt the completeness of the gift to effect the purposes of the giver!—would thaw the iced feelings of her father, and tune his heart to the song of forgiveness. Yet, it was not without many fears, and tears, and misgivings, on the part of the maiden, that they began their march for the Maha village. The lover, now a stranger to fear, used his endeavours to quiet the beautiful Tatoka, and in some measure succeeded.

Upon finding that his daughter and her lover had gone to the Hill of the Spirits, and that Shongotongo did not return from his perilous adventure, the chief of the Mahas had recalled his Braves from the pursuit, and was listening to the history of the pair, as far as the returned warriors were acquainted with it, when his daughter and her lover made their appearance. With a bold and fearless step the once faint-hearted Karkapaha walked up to the offended father, and, folding his arms on his breast, stood erect as a pine, and motionless as that tree when the winds of the earth are chained above the clouds. It was the first time that Karkapaha had ever looked on angry men without trembling, and a demeanour so unusual in him excited universal surprise.

"Karkapaha is a thief," said the White Crane.

"It is the father of my beautiful and beloved Tatoka that says it," answered the lover; "else would Karkapaha say it was the song of a bird that has flown over."

"My warriors say it."

"Your warriors are singing-birds; they are wrens; Karkapaha says they do not speak the truth.—Karkapaha has the heart of a tiger, and the strength of a bear; let the Braves try him. He has thrown away the woman's heart; he has become a man."

"Karkapaha *is* changed," said the chief thoughtfully, "but when, and how?"

"The Little Spirits of the Mountain have given him a new soul. Bid your Braves draw this bow; bid them poise this spear. Their eyes say they can do neither. Then is Karkapaha the strong man of his tribe;" and as he said this he flourished the ponderous spear over his head as a man would poise a reed, and drew the bow as a child would bend a willow twig.

"Karkapaha is the husband of Tatoka," said Mahtoree, springing to his feet, and he gave the beautiful maiden to her lover. The traditionary lore of the Mahas is full of the exploits, both in war and the chase, of Karkapaha, who was made a man by the Spirits of the Mountain.

THE VALLEY OF THE BRIGHT OLD INHABITANTS.

On the northern branch of the river of the Cherokees, the most numerous and powerful tribe of the south, there are two high mountains nearly covered with mossy rocks, and lofty cedars, and pines. These mountains, rugged and terrible to behold, are made yet more fearful to the mind of the red man of the forest, who sees the Great Being in the clouds, and hears him in the winds, and fancies a spirit in every thing that moves, by the horrid sights and awful sounds which proceed from them. Often, as the sun sinks behind those mountains, persons who have their eyes intently fixed upon them will see lofty forms whose heads stretch far into the sky, standing upon their summits, or oftener leaping from one mountain to the other clean across the wide valley which separates them. Those shapes we can see wear the shape of man, yet their actions do not seem to belong to a race of mortals, and we deem them spirits — giant spirits, which never had the sinews, and bones, and muscle, and flesh, of men. And often, in the midnight hour, the listener hears sounds proceeding from those mountains — the whispers of love, the loud tones of strife, or the merry ones of joy — laughing and weeping — wooing and strife — expressing all the various passions and emotions which find a place in the bosoms of mortals. With these mighty spirits no mortal hath had communication, for they never leave the mountain — and who shall dare approach their villages? No one has heard their story, no one knows their creator, nor when they were born, nor when they shall die, if death be appointed to them. They have lived in mystery: showing their forms as the trunk of a decayed, and branch-less tree shows itself from out a morning mist, and raising their voices but as a thunder-cloud in summer, they will depart as a spirit departs, noiselessly, and go no one knows whither.

Between these two lofty and dreaded mountains, there is a deep valley, or rather a succession of deep valleys, for the occurrence at short spaces of low hills breaks the continuousness of that with which the space between those mountains commences. In these valleys the beams of the sun are concentrated and drawn together, creating at times a heat so great, that nothing can live in them but those reptiles, which are ripened and fattened to full growth only by suns which scorch like fire. In these same valleys have dwelt, ever since the earth was first placed on the back of the great tortoise, those Kind Old Kings, the *Bright Old Inhabitants*(1), which are rattle-snakes of a most prodigious size, possessed of singular properties, and endowed with tremendous and fearful powers. It is death to venture within their limits, and equally fatal to displease them. So well convinced are the people of my nation of their power to inflict an instant and dreadful death on all, that no temptation can induce them to betray their secret recesses to the wanton stranger. They well know that, if they do so, they shall be exposed to the unceasing attacks of all the inferior species of snakes who love their kings, which are these Bright Old Inhabitants, and know by instinct those who injure, or attempt to injure them. They know that, let but those kings issue their commands, there is not a snake that crawls but will open his mouth or use his sting to inflict the greatest possible degree of vengeance in his power on the enemies and oppressors of those whom he loves and obeys. Hence the place of residence of the Kind Old Kings is kept a secret by our people. For a long time they did not know it themselves, and only became acquainted with it when the occurrence took place which I am about to relate to my brother.

Once upon a time, many years ago, there lived among the Cherokees a man who was neither a warrior nor a hunter, yet was the most celebrated man of his nation, and further known than its proudest warrior or most expert hunter. He was a priest, and knew the secret ways, and the will, and the wishes, of his master, the Great Spirit. Not only was he skilled in the wisdom of the land of souls, but he was learned in matters which affect the dwellers in the body. He knew how to cure the ailments of the body, as well as to give answers to the questions which related to the ways and doings of the Being above all. He could tell at what time in the morning men should go to the Hill of Prayer, with clay on their heads, to cry for mercy and aid, and when they should repair to the Cave of Sacrifice, to gather the will of the Great Spirit from the hollow voice [27] within it. He alone, of all the mighty nation of the Cherokees, had seen that Spirit; he alone had heard him speak, and to none other would that Spirit deign to listen, or to give reply. Chepiasquit, for that was the name of this famous priest, was indeed a very wise man, and his sayings were reckoned of scarcely less authority then the words of his master. Whatever he said had a weight which other men's words had not; and all his actions, however trifling in their nature, were magnified into actions of importance, and became invested with a character, which did not belong to those of men in other respects more gifted than he. Yet the unbounded respect in which his nation held him was not undeserved. Wisdom he possessed, and he used it to the furthering of the interests, and the advancing of the happiness, of his people. If they wanted rain, they asked Chepiasquit for it, and he gave it to them. If too much fell, they had only to complain to him, and the clouds witheld their floods, and the waters were locked up in the hollow of the hand of him that created them. If the thunders were heard to roll awfully, and the fearful lightnings were seen to flash along the black sky, they spoke to Chepiasquit, who uttered a short prayer to Him who controuls the elements as well as man, and all became hushed and still; the black clouds passed away, and the bright stars looked out from their places of rest in the clear blue sky. All things seemed obedient to him, when he chose to open his lips in supplication to his master. The fame which he had acquired by this intimacy and friendship with the Great Spirit was the means of giving peace to his nation. His reputation being spread far and near, no tribe durst try their strength in war, or measure their weapons in combat, with a people who were possessed of such a friend, protector, leader, and priest. So the Cherokees rested in peace, and the earth was no more made red with blood, but wore the robe which nature provided for it—the robe of green. They planted their corn in the Budding-Moon, and lived to see it harvested in the Moon of Falling Leaves. They left the doors of their cabins unlatched at night, and the sentinel slept as sound and as long as the new-born babe. Their arrows were eaten up by the rust of sloth and inactivity, and the strings of their bows were rotted by the mildew of carelessness and idleness. The aged met not now in the great council-house, to plan distant expeditions, or frustrate expected invasions; the youth spent their time in court-ing and marrying. The fame of Chepiasquit changed the character of the nation from warlike to peaceable, and banished from the land the vulture of war and havoc, to give place to the dove of peace and tranquillity.

Four wives had this wise priest; they bore him many children: but, great as was his power with the Master of the World, it did not enable him to obtain for them a continuance of life beyond the se-cond moon of their birth. All, save one, died while they were yet swinging in their cradles of willow-bark from the bough of the tree—that one, a daughter, was spared to his entreaties and prayers. Winona, or the first-born, for that was the name bestowed on the child, grew up in the cabin of her father, beautiful beyond any maiden that ever graced the nation of Cherokees. How shall I de-scribe to my brother from the far country the matchless charms of Chepiasquit's virgin daughter! Shall I tell him that her eyes were the eyes of the mountain kid, and her hair long and glossier than the plumage of the raven, and her teeth white and even, and her hand delicate and plump, and her foot small and speedy? Shall I say that her voice was joyful as the voice of a mated bird in spring, and her temper cheerful, sweet, mild, kind, and always the same? Shall I increase his admiration for the beautiful creature, by telling him that she best loved to sit by the quiet hearth of her parents, leaving it to lighter and less amiable maidens to rove on idle errands and frivolous pursuits through the village. For, let my brother learn, she was that wonder, a woman, contented and happy in her own house, with none but her own father to listen or reply. During the long evenings of the period when the sun is away from the earth for so great a portion of the day, she would sit on her soft couch of skins and dried moss, listening to the tales he would repeat of the wonderful things he had seen and heard; the dreams of strange and fearful creatures which had troubled his hours of sleep, and the actual appearance to him, when sleep was far from his eyelids, of beings or phantoms not of this world; and the traditions which told of the love, or hatred, or favour, or punishment, of the Great Spirit—of his bounties sent to the Cherokees, when famine reared his gaunt form among them, or of wrath provoked, and punishment inflicted, when pride dwelt in their villages, when their thoughts were far from him, when no clay was put on their heads, when the tender and juicy flesh of the deer smoked not in his sacrifice. Wars he had seen, though he had left victory to be achieved by others, for he had been a man of peace. To the tales of her beloved father would the fair maiden listen with great delight, for they accorded with the belief in wonderful events and supernatural appearances, which is early impressed on the mind of every Indian, and never leaves him but with life. She would sit for hours with her little head rested on her palm, her whole soul absorbed by the wild narratives, which, during the long season of winter, are related to while away the hours spared from war and the chace.

Beloved with a greater degree of affection than is usually felt even among those whose lives are little subject to the incidents which weaken or destroy attachments, the beautiful daughter of the Cherokee priest grew up to womanhood, the cherished idol of all her friends, the boast and pride of the nation. The young and ardent

Braves sought her hand in marriage; but she was deaf to all their entreaties and protestations, and refused all their offers. Yet she did it with so much kindness, and said so many sweet words to blunt the severity of the refusal, that all her lovers became her friends, and each, with affectionate kindness, blended with the bold bearing of one who says what he knows he has courage to perform, promised that his love mellowed into friendship should remain firmly fixed in his heart, and that he would defend its object, should danger cross her path, as long as strength was given him to carry a spear. The rejection by the fair Winona of so many youths, most of whom were deemed worthy of her choice, gave the father pain; but he loved his daughter too well to wish to make her unhappy by a marriage with one she did not love. He had seen—and who does not?—that the bird selects for its mate the bird it likes best; that love and affection go to the pairing of all creatures, save man and woman; and that only with them is it a practice to bind together, and fetter for life, those whose hearts are far apart. And he knew, that the Great Spirit disliked that force or constraint should be used in affairs of this kind. So, in obedience to the will of his master, as well as the dictates of his own reason, and the affection he bore her, he permitted his lovely and gentle child to remain unmarried in his house.

But it was not decreed by him who governs all things that the beautiful maiden should always remain a stranger to the delightful pains and agonising pleasures of love. It was in the second month of spring, when all nature feels the influence of the returning sun, when birds are carolling on every spray, and the grass and flowers are waking up from their long and chilled, sleep, and the joyous deer is out to nip the young buds, that a company of young hunters from the distant but far-famed nation of the Muscogulgees, passing through the lands of the Cherokees, stopped for rest and refreshment, and to try the strength of our young men in the exercises which youth love, at the village in which the father of the beautiful maiden abode. These young hunters were the flower of that valiant nation, bred up to pursue with equal courage and ardour the savage bear into his fearful retreats, and the foe, notwithstanding his treacherous ambuscades, through the dark and almost impervious forest. War was their natural and most beloved pursuit; but now they had doffed their martial habiliments, wiped off their war-paint, and taken up the bow and spear to pursue the peaceful occupation of hunting. The leader of this youthful band of Muscogulgees, was a tall and stately youth, formed in the noblest and most animated mould of the human form, straight as a young cedar, with eyes that indicated the fire of his soul, and brow, and cheek, and lip, that showed the mildness of his heart. With a small eagle feather, the badge of his chieftainship in his hair, his robe of dressed deer-skin thrown lightly over his shoulder, at which hung his bow and well filled quiver, he walked among the admiring youths and maidens of our nation, a thing to be feared, dreaded, and loved. He and his company of chosen young Braves now received the welcome, and experienced, the hospitality, which, in every situation, and at every season, the red man of the forest offers to those who visit him. They were feasted and caressed by each and all. The painted pole was erected and the feast prepared, that an opportunity might be afforded them of recounting their exploits in the ears of the listening Braves of our nation; the wrestling ring was formed, that their skill and strength, if they possessed such, in that exercise, might be shown; games of chance were appointed, that the favour of the Great Spirit, and the strength of the protecting *okkis* of each nation and individual, might be demonstrated. In every undertaking, was the superior skill and strength of the youthful leader of the Muscogulgee band made apparent. In the wrestling ring, the strongest man of the Cherokees was but a child in his hands; his voice, in the song of his own exploits, and the recital of the glories of his nation, was sweeter than the sighing of the gentlest spring wind, and clearer than the prattling music of the waterfall. In the games which were played he was equally successful, and he rose from the *match of straws* winner of half the valued treasures and trophies of the opposing Braves. Was it strange, that one so bold and brave should ingratiate himself with the beautiful maidens of our tribe? Was it strange, that bright eyes should glisten with tears, and soft bosoms be filled with throbs, and red lips be fraught with sighs, when the Guard of the Red Arrows passed before the eyes of beauty? Was it any thing to excite especial wonder, that the beautiful daughter of the priest should suffer the fires of love to be lit in her tender bosom? or that the valiant and handsome Muscogulgee should think her the fairest creature he had ever seen, should reciprocate the soft passion which glowed in her bosom, and wish to transfer the lovely flower of the Cherokees from the cabin of her father to his distant home?

The Guard of the Red Arrows said to the father of the maiden, "I love your daughter. Her bright black eyes, and long black locks, her melodious voice, and her gentleness, and her sweet temper, and her winning air, have caught my heart, as a bird is entangled in the snare of the fowler, or a deer entrapped in the toils of the hunter. She has become the light of my soul—when I see her not, all is darkness. I have no eyes but for her; my ears drink in no other accents than hers; my last thought when I sink to rest is of the beautiful Fawn, my first when I awake of the bright-eyed little maiden who gits by the cabin-fire of the wise priest of her nation. I hare opened my heart to this charming maiden, and have heard from her lips a soft confession of her love for the Muscogulgee. She consents to leave the house of her father, and the home of her childhood, to go, with the Guard of the Red Arrows, to the cabin he has built himself beside the beautiful and rapid river of his nation."

The father answered, "I cannot spare my daughter to go to the far home of him who asks her hand. She is the light of my eyes, and the joy of my heart. What would her mother say, and how should I answer the fond questions which, with eyes streaming with tears, she would ask, if I permitted the little fawn she has nursed with so much care to go forth to a distant land—to be in the morning of her youth separated from all her friends and companions, and taken to a new and unknown abode? Gloom would be in my cabin, and tears would rush from the eyes, that for seventeen harvests have been accustomed to see the gentle maiden performing her acts of dutiful kindness, and gliding with a foot noiseless as snow around the couches of her beloved parents. We should listen in the morning for the carol of the sweetest of all birds, and miss in the evening the tread of the lightest mortal foot that ever brushed the dew from the flowers of the prairie. There would be one missing from the repast of meat; one from the dance of maidens beneath the shady oak; one from the couch of moss where we sleep. No, Muscogulgee! I cannot spare the fawn. How should I answer the fond questions of her mother, when, with eyes streaming with tears, she should ask me for her daughter? When I told her the truth, she would cry, 'Hard and cruel man! thou hast torn from me the darling of my heart, the idol of my soul. — What shall become of me — of thee, thus deprived of our sweet child?' No, Muscogulgee! I must refuse thee my daughter. And yet, if thou wilt renounce thine own nation, and come and take up thy residence in the native land of her thou lovest, or pretendest to love, the maiden shall be thine. Thou shalt have a cabin built beside my own, and, as is our Indian wont, the friends of thy bride shall place within it all the household implements needed in our simple life. Her friends shall be thy friends, and her father thy father, and her mother thy mother. When there is thunder and darkness in the sky of the Cherokees, it shall thunder and be dark in the sky of the Muscogulgee sojourner among them, and with whomsoever the Cherokees have buried the hatchet of war, and made a league of amity, with that tribe or people shall the Muscogulgee keep terms of peace."

The Muscogulgee answered, as became him, that "his father, and his mother, and his brothers, and his sisters, and all the friends of his youth, were dwelling in the land of his birth — the land of his father's bones — how could he quit it? Why should he fly his fatherland, a land pleasant to look upon, and healthful to live in, abounding in quiet glades where the deer loved to browze, in pleasant streams filled with fish, in smooth and tranquil lakes, fanned by the wings of the innumerable fowls which went thither for food. Much as he loved the beautiful flower of the Cherokees, and much as he wished to make her his bride, he could not become an exile to obtain her. Why should her father object to her following the steps of him she loved, and who would be unto her father, mother, sister, brother, friend, in that one word *husband*?"

And thus pleaded the lover, but he pleaded in vain, for the father remained deaf to his entreaties and prayers. Not so the daughter. She had drunk the sweet poison of his words, and, when he clasped her to his breast, felt that there was more bliss in that clasp than could be communicated by the kindest words, and fondest looks, and richest gifts, of those who were the authors of her being. She heard his fond words, and believed them true; she saw his face, and knew it fair, and she trusted him. It was agreed between them, that when the moon had hid herself behind the lofty woods which skirted the village of her birth, she should fly from the house of her father, with the Guard of the Red Arrows, to the cabin he had built him beside the beautiful river of his nation. But they forgot—these fond and foolish lovers!—that the Great Spirit was the friend of Chepiasquit, and made him acquainted with all the secret doings of those who would harm him, or interfere with his family concerns. They forgot,—simple children!—that the wise powwow had but to feel the stirring of the ant under the skin of the left hand, when, binding over his eyes the hide of a young badger, and laying his head upon a pillow composed of the leaves of the black hornbeam, the Manitou of Dreams would make known to him every machination of his enemies. The plans of the youthful pair for flight were soon revealed to the cunning powwow by his faithful spirit, and he arose in the morning, knowing what the night would bring forth, and fully prepared to punish the attempts which were to be made against the peace of his family. He made all those careful preparations for impending danger which a wise and prudent chief should make. He shut up his daughter in his lodge, and, calling around him the Braves of his nation, he made them acquainted with the designs of the Muscogulgee, and bade them keep guard around the endangered cabin and its coveted treasure, but on no account—if it could be dispensed with—to do harm to the strangers. Having prepared to oppose violence by violence, if need should be, he, wishing to prevent bloodshed, for he was a man of peace, called to him the lover of his daughter, and addressed him thus:

"I did say thou couldst not have my daughter, but upon one condition—I recall my word, and add thereto a second. She shall be, with the consent of her father, the companies of thy homeward journey, if thy heart be strong enough to undertake one quest, and it be the will of the Great Spirit that thou be spared to accomplish it. Let the valiant Muscogulgee, who has man written on his brow and eye, though the down on his cheek proclaims him boy, listen to the words of the father of Winona, and remember that the manifestation of a strong heart, at this time, may avail much to gain him the object he so ardently covets.

"Between the two mountains which rear their lofty heads on the northern branch of the river of the Cherokees, there is a deep valley, in which the beams of the sun, being concentrated and drawn together, create a heat so insupportable that nothing can live there but those reptiles, which are ripened and fattened to full growth only by fervid and burning suns. In these deep valleys have dwelt, ever since the beginning of the world, those Bright Old Inhabitants, the chiefs and fathers of the rattlesnakes, who are called by our nation the "Kind Old Kings," being, indeed, the sovereigns of all the tribes or species of snakes to be found on the earth. It has been death to venture within their limits, and almost as fatal to displease them by speaking ill of them, or by harming any of their subjects. Hence we know nothing of their villages, or their numbers, or their policy — whether they die like ourselves, or if the copy of nature be eternal in them. These things would I know; but above all would I know if the lights which shine so transcendently in those valleys be, as many say, the eyes of those Kind Old Kings, or be substances not connected with them — precious stones lit up by the beams of the sun, or dazzling meteors shining by their own light. Go, brave young man, visit this valley; confer with the wise old reptiles that inhabit it: above all see if the lights which illumine it be the eyes of those snakes, or dazzling meteors shining by their own light, or precious stones lit up by the beams of the sun. And thou must bring me a tooth from the jaw of a living king, and a rattle from his tail, and an eye from his skull. When thou shalt bring us an account of these things, the hand of my daughter shall accompany her heart, and the one shall become, as the other hath been, the property of the valiant Muscogulgee. But, until thou hast performed the required task, my daughter remains guarded in my cabin."

The Muscogulgee heard the words of the father, and grief filled his soul. He had heard — for who in those wilds was ignorant of the tradition? — of the "bright old inhabitants," and he knew how deadly the enmity which they bear to those who trespass upon their sacred and secluded retreats. He knew that, in undertaking this invasion of their solitudes, small chance remained to him of escaping death from their dreadful fangs. Though they were called the Kind Old Kings, they were known not to deserve that appellation when just cause was given for anger. These considerations presented themselves to the young Muscogulgee, but they did not appal him. He loved the beautiful daughter of the priest, and, deeming that life passed without her would not be worth possessing, he determined to attempt the task which would end it, or give to his arms the object of his love, the bright and blooming Cherokee maiden. So he made answer to Chepiasquit, that he would do, or attempt to do, the thing required of him, and received from the wise old *powwow* a renewal of his promise, that the maiden should be his when his task should be accomplished. Then, turning to his companions, who had gathered around him, he bade them return immediately to the land of the Muscogulgees, and impart to his friends a knowledge of the hazardous expedition which he had undertaken. And then, in the presence of her father and mother, he bade adieu to the blushing maiden, who received, with many tears, the kiss of affection upon her soft cheek, and raised her wet eyes in speechless prayer to the Great Spirit that he might be returned to her arms.

The powwow said to the Muscogulgee, "Thou hast undertaken a fearful thing, and one which I warn thee will require much and deep thought and caution, and great valour and wisdom. Thou shalt have my aid and counsel, but they may not avail so much as thine own steadiness of soul, and strength of arm. Nevertheless, I will give thee a charm, a potent charm, and see thou rememberest my directions for its use."

So saying, he drew forth from his basket of amulets the skin of a mountain cat, in which was a medicine, compounded of those powerful substances which nature furnishes, to enable men to acquire command over their own and the inferior species. There were the vine which never bore fruit, the dry cones of the pine, steeped in the dew that drops from the leaves of the mountain-laurel, the claws of the tiger, the teeth of the alligator, the thighbone of the tortoise, and the ribs of the snail, reduced to a powder, and mixed up with water dropped from the shell of the butternut, through the ochre of war. The wise master of the spell had drawn from field, and forest, earth, air, and water, from beast and bird, and fish and reptile, and insect and tree, and flower and fruit, all the various properties which have an agency in subduing things to the will of him, to whom those properties have been taught. From these he had compounded a medicine, the mighty power of which was unknown even to himself. Placing this amulet in the hands of the wondering youth, he bade him remember to repeat aloud the following words, and in the following manner, should he deem there was occasion for its use. "I am lost! I am lost! save me! save me! In the name of the seven men that were bewildered in a foggy morning, and cooked for the breakfast of the Kind Old Kings, I call upon thee, Maiden in Green, to protect me from the like fate." The youthful lover received the sacred amulet, with all the reverence which it ought to inspire, and, before the great star of day had sunk to sleep behind the hills of the west, he had slung his bow and quiver to his shoulder, and taken up the line of his march to the fated valley.

Travelling onward with great expedition, he came near the close of the next day to the entrance of the eventful spot. He saw the high mountains covered with mossy rocks, and tall cedars, and pines, and beheld the "lofty forms, whose heads stretched far into the sky," and heard the sounds which proceeded from their lips, the soft whispers of love, the loud tones of strife, or the merry ones of joy, laughing and weeping, wooing and strife, signs that they were possessed of the various passions and emotions which find a place in the breasts of mortals. Between these mountains lay the deep valley spoken of, but what it was which glittered and glistened in it, he knew not. Whatever it was, it shone with a splendour which eclipsed the meridian beams of the sun. The whole space between the two mountains seemed a glare of light, which dazzled even more than the fiercest glare of noon in the Month of Thunder. What still more astonished and perplexed the youth was, that the light seemed of various colours, ever changing, never for a moment wearing the same appearance. Now it wore the hue of the maple leaf in autumn, now of the tuft of the blue heron—now it was purple, now green, now yellow, and then it seemed a mixture of them all, a blending of all the colours ever beheld into one. Astonished and dismayed, but still determined to win the hand of the beautiful Winona or perish, the Guard of the Red Arrows undauntedly entered the valley, and approached the scene of wondrous splendour. Moving with great difficulty, for the entrance was overrun with briars and many other vicious impediments, he came all at once to a clear field, and beheld what had so enchanted and spell-bound at a distance—what so filled with horror now it was nearer beheld. He saw the earth covered with rattlesnakes of a more enormous size than any ever beheld by man, ay, beyond what even his imagination had pictured in his most restless and diseased hours of sleep. The bodies of many of them were larger than the trunks of the largest forest trees, and so unwieldy that, when they would turn round, they were compelled to take a circle almost as wide as their length. But bountiful nature, which always compensates for a defect or disadvantage by adding an excellence, made up for the heavy motion of their bodies by bestowing upon them the power of irresistible fascination. She gave to them an eye—to each a single eye—placing it in the centre of their foreheads, possessing the power to draw to them every living creature. It was this eye which emitted the wonderful light which had so dazzled the Muscogulgee at a distance, and still more dazzled now that he was within reach of the horrid fascination. These eyes were of every possible colour, and the light they sent forth was as various as the colour of the eyes. Nor could the colour of any one of those eyes be set down as positively this or that, for each moment was it changing. Now the green eye became blue as the midnight sky—look again, it was yellow as the fallen leaf; a fourth time, the scarlet hue was entering upon one side, while the yellow was retreating from the other, leaving the middle a strange combination of both. Long might the Muscogulgee have gazed on the brilliant, but terrible scene—a field, stretching farther than the eye could reach, and all covered with immense snakes, hissing with a sound loud as the roar of the tempest, shaking their rattles with a noise like thunder, the while their eyes emitted the light which he shuddered to look at, and yet, such was their power of fascination, he was unable to turn from—long, I repeat, might he have gazed on the scene, but he found himself irresistibly impelled to enter the field of light. His feet were irresistibly drawn forward, his mouth was opened to deprecate the anger of the Great Being, his hands were upraised at what he knew must be instant destruction, for already were their dreadful jaws expanded, and their hideous tongues, red as burning coals, twinkling with a motion so quick that it seemed but the soul of a vapour, when he bethought himself of the charm given to him by the wise priest, and drew it forth. Bowing, as he was bidden, to the spirit of storms, who rules the east, to the kind genius of the south, to the master of the west wind, and to the North Star, which is the best friend of hunters and bewildered men, he thrice called upon the Great Spirit, crying in a loud voice, "I am lost! I am lost! save me! save me! In the name of the seven men who were bewildered in a foggy morning, and cooked for the breakfast of the Kind Old Kings, I call upon thee, Maiden in Green, to protect me from a like fate." Is my brother prepared to hear what was the effect produced by these words? Does he wish to know if that shrill cry called up a being unable to protect him, or if the rattles were stilled, and the jaws were closed, and if darkness was imparted to those glittering eyes, and silence to those wicked tongues? Listen.

There came to the ears of the Muscogulgee youth, from the summit of the Northern mountains, a sound of distant thunder, which in a moment was succeeded by the sweetest song that ever was breathed upon mortal ears. He could not distinguish all the words, but he heard enough to teach him that it was a song of supplication to the Great Spirit for a "brave and good Muscogulgee hunter, about to be caught in the fangs of the Kind Old Kings." The moment the thunder and the song were heard, the rattles were still, the bright eyes sent forth no more light, and the fiery tongues retreated within the closed and recumbent jaws. Of all that body of hideous reptiles not one seemed to be imbued with breath. Nearer and nearer came the song, and as it came the hunter fancied that it was the music of a being moving level with the earth, if not beneath its surface. He was right. Soon, in the grass at his feet, appeared a little snake scarcely thicker than his little finger, and not longer than the space between his hand and his shoulder. The colours of this little reptile were as various and beautiful as those of the eyes of the Kind Old Kings, but these were fixed and permanent, those as I have said changeable and changing as a woman's mind. The head was green, the sides were yellow, the belly white, down its back ran two red stripes, and there were rings of bright crimson around its tail. Elevating its head as it drew near, it remained stationary and silent for a moment, and then addressed the Muscogulgee in these words: —

"I am the spirit raised by the potent *medicine* of the Cherokee priest; and, invoked by thy call, I have hastened hither at thy cry of distress, to tell thee thou art not *lost*. Though thou didst a foolish thing to come to this valley of death, and he, at whose bidding the thing was undertaken, a wicked one in sending thee, yet thou shalt not die this time. I am the Maiden in Green, the ruling Spirit of both mountain and valley, having power over even the Bright Old Inhabitants, and they shall not harm thee. Thou art, if I remember right, commanded, as the price of the beautiful daughter of the Cherokee *powwow*, to carry to him a tooth from the jaw of a living King and a rattle from his tail, and an eye from his skull; and to report of sundry things not necessary to be named. Thou shalt have my aid to accomplish these things."

So saying, the Maiden in Green re-commenced her song, the while making a circuit around the prisoner at a small distance from him. When she had finished the circuit, she changed her song to one which seemed a song of reproach and threatening. Whatever was the subject, it had the effect of rekindling the Bright Old Inhabitants to their former state of wrath. Their eyes were relit with the glittering beams, and the hissing and the rattling re-commenced. Seemingly determined to take instant vengeance upon the intruder, they were now seen making such haste as their natural tardiness admitted of, towards the Muscogulgee. From every part of the valley heads could be seen displaying forked tongues, and all pressing towards the alarmed warrior. But he stood invulnerable to them, though he knew it not, within the charmed circle made by his protecting spirit. Their powers of fascination had been taken away by the Maiden in Green, or rather the counter-fascination, which kept him within the charmed space, was more powerful than the influence of their eyes.

Calling to one of the largest of the Kind Old Kings to come near, the Maiden in Green spoke to him thus: — "This youth is a brave youth, and he is a Muscogulgee. He loves the beautiful daughter of the *powwow* Chepiasquit, and has asked her of her father to wife. The father has imposed on him the task to visit your valley, and make report whether your eyes are dazzling meteors, or precious stones. And he has bidden him bring a tooth from the jaw of a living King, and a rattle from his tail, and an eye from his skull, the which, being faithfully and fully accomplished, entitles him to claim, as a pledged boon, the hand of the lovely Winona. What say you, chief of the kings, shall he return and be made happy?"

The chief of the kings answered that he knew of no one who would willingly spare an eye, or a tooth, or a rattle. For himself, he had found them all of use, and could spare neither eye, tooth, nor rattle. And he bade the Spirit remember, that though queen of both valley and mountain, her sway extended but to protect, and not to injure. She had no right to demand from the Kind Old Kings a thing which should inflict pain or death upon them. And did she not know that, whenever one of those eyes of light should be carried beyond the limits of the valley, the transcendent power and brightness which their owners now possessed should be enjoyed by them no more. Such was the will of the Great Being; strange that the Maiden in Green should be ignorant of it.

The Spirit answered that she knew not this, yet she was prepared to say that the decree should be revoked, if they would, without any further molestation, impart to the Muscogulgee the required information, and bestow upon him the gift which would make him happy and prosperous in his suit to the Cherokee maiden. Should they favour his request, brilliancy should be added to, rather than taken from, their eyes, and their rattles should grow in size, and increase in number and speed of motion. But, if they refused to grant him the boon, the eye, and the tooth, and the rattle, should be taken from them by force, whereby they would lose the benefit of having done something to be thanked for.

Upon hearing this, the chief of the Wise Old Kings called a council of his nation. I know not what was said in this council, but I can tell my brother what was done. They drew lots among them, and he upon whom the lot fell submitted to lose an eye, and a tooth, and a rattle. Having given these to the Muscogulgee, the eldest of the Kings instructed him in their history, their laws, and their policy, replying particularly to the questions suggested by the Cherokee *powwow*.

"We were created," said he, "after all the other beings were created, and were formed from the variegated sand which is found on the shores of the distant Lake of the Woods. It was in a pleasant and sunny morning in the Buck-Moon, that the Great Spirit, having nothing else to do, amused himself, as he sat in the warm sun on the bank of this lake, with twisting ropes of those parti-coloured sands. Having twisted, in mere sport, a considerable number, and laid them aside, it came to his mind that amidst all the variety of creatures he had formed, whose means of locomotion were walking, flying, swimming, hopping, trotting, running, there were none ordained to move altogether by crawling. 'Now,' said he to himself, 'if

I were breathe into these ropes the breath of life, and to invest them with the power to run about, would it not be a sight worth seeing? — would it not create a deal of sport among the other animals? But I will make them more wonderful yet.'

"So saying, he selected a number of small round stones, of which he thrust several into one end of the ropes. Before him, upon the shore, were scattered many stones of different hues, but all of surpassing brilliancy, and each outshining the beams of the meridian sun. He placed one of these shining gems in the other end of each rope, and then blew upon them until they exhibited signs of life. When the ropes began to move, their strange and zigzag motions, and the rattling of their tails, excited the mirth of the Great Being, who laughed loud and long at the oddity he had formed. That portion of them to which he had given rattles and the shining eye were appointed rulers over all the other and inferior species of snakes. And he bade them remember that he had formed them to crawl in the dust all the days of their lives, and on no account to attempt an upright posture. 'But,' said he, as he concluded the word which bade them be ever of the dust, 'this is no place for your tribes. Ye are a thin-skinned, or rather a skinless race, and should have a habitation and a name only where fervid suns beam, and the frosts and snows of winter are little known. Ye could never reach that land if left to your own exertions — I must assist you.' So saying, he gathered all the new-born reptiles into his hand, and, hiding them in the folds of his robe, took his departure towards the warm regions of the South. A few hours sufficed to bring him to the valley which we now occupy, and here he committed us, and all the tribes over which we are appointed rulers, to the fostering care of the bright and glorious star of day. Having created us, and breathed into us the breath of life, he bade us, as he had done all the other creatures, each, for the future, to provide for his own wants. We who carried the rattles were to live for ever; all the others were to die at an appointed time. We were commanded never to leave the valley, and, as a compensation for being restricted in our walks, we were to exercise for ever dominion over all the other species of snakes. And, as a protection from those who might wage a war of invasion against us, our eyes were gifted with the power to fascinate, and attract to us, every living creature that came within the scope of their vision, save those who were specially favoured by the Spirit of the Mountain. And thus it is. We, the Kind Old Kings, are the identical ropes of sand which were twisted in the beginning of the world by the Maker of all; those of small stature, which ye see around us, are our children, and the children of our children. *They* die, but to us who carry the dazzling eyes, death is not appointed. Yet we increase in stature, and shall continue increasing in stature, till the Great Tortoise upon which the earth reposes shall sink into the endless abyss of waters, carrying with him that earth and all its numerous creatures.

"You may thank the Spirit of the Mountain, Muscogulgee, for your life. It was forfeited, and would have been taken, but for the intervention of the Maiden in Green. You may now return—the bearer of what never before left the valley of the Bright Old Inhabitants—an eye, and a tooth, and a rattle—wisdom gathered from my words, and instruction from my lips. They shall not avail him for whom they are intended, since their possession would convey to him a power which the Great Spirit would not—could not, without danger to himself—permit a mortal to exercise. I hand you a tooth: already does the great *powwow* of the Cherokees feel, with the increase of the strength of his mind, the decrease of the strength of his body: here is the rattle, his strength is ebbing away; the eye, I behold him helpless on the bed of death. His face is bright with the wisdom and knowledge imparted by the gifts he hath obtained from us, but, alas! his tongue is nerveless, he may not communicate the knowledge he hath gained. Hasten back in peace, Muscogulgee, deliver to him the gifts which seal his fate and thine—his, to die ere the moon be two days older—thine, to gain the maiden thou so ardently longest for, and with her to descend the stream of time, loving and beloved—the happiest of the happy. But, remember, let none of thy race or name presume again to visit this valley, lest the most dreadful fate be theirs."

So spoke the eldest of the Wise Old Kings, and his words were repeated by all his brothers. They permitted the Muscogulgee to depart in peace, and he returned to the village of the Cherokee priest. He delivered the gifts as he had been directed, and witnessed the end he had been taught to expect. He saw the countenance of the *powwow* lighted up with intelligence more than mortal, but, at the delivery of each gift, he beheld a third part of the vigour of animal life fade away, as the eye, the bright, the unfading, but fatal eye, was placed in his trembling hand, he saw the spark of life quivering like a lamp in the socket. The priest had just time to beckon to him his lovely daughter, when, placing her hand in that of the Muscogulgee youth, he expired.

Brother, I am a Muscogulgee, and my mother was the beautiful daughter of the Cherokee priest, and my father the brave youth who adventured into the valley of the Bright Old Inhabitants. I have done.

NOTE.

(1) *Valley of the Bright Old Inhabitants.* — p. 225.

Several of the Indian nations believe themselves descended from rattlesnakes, and all, more or less, profess relationship with that reptile. A Seneca chief told me that his maternal ancestor was a maiden rattlesnake, but he destroyed the sublimity of the fiction by asserting that on their nuptial night she bit off her husband's nose.

Heckewelder, after remarking that some of the Tuscaroras claim affinity with the rabbit and the ground hog, says: "I found also that the Indians, for a similar reason, paid great respect to the rattle-snake, whom they called their *grandfather*, and would on no account destroy him. One day, as I was walking with an elderly Indian on the banks of the Muskingum, I saw a large rattlesnake lying across the path, which I was going to kill. The Indian immediately forbade my doing so, 'for,' said he, 'the rattlesnake is grandfather to the In-dians, and is placed here on purpose to guard us, and to give us warning of impending danger by his rattles, which is the same as if he were to tell us 'Look about!' 'Now, added he,' if we were to kill one of those, the others would soon know it, and the whole race would rise upon us, and bite us.' I observed to him that the white people were not afraid of this, for they killed all the rattlesnakes they met with. On this he enquired whether any white man had been bitten by those animals, and of course I answered in the af-firmative. 'No wonder, then,' he replied, 'you have to blame your-selves for that. Take care you do not irritate them in our country, they and their grandchildren are on good terms, and neither will hurt the other.'"

Adair, after killing one which infested the camp of the Seminoles, found himself in serious danger, whereupon he remarks in a note page 263, that the Seminoles "never kill the rattlesnake."

THE LEGEND OF MOSHUP.

The sound or strait, which divides Nope [28] from the main land and the islands of Nashawn, was not, in the days of our fathers, so wide as it is now. The small bays which now indent the northern shore of Nope, and the slight promontories, which, at intervals of a mile or two, jut out along its coast of a sun's journey, were then wanting; neither the one nor the other obtruded on its round and exact outline. The strong current of waters from the boundless bosom of the Great Lake, sweeping down between this island and the opposite little islands of Nashawn and its sisters, has made great encroachments upon the former, widening to a journey of two hours what was once only the work of one to perform. My brothers, who are with me from the lands of the Pawkunnawkuts, know that my words are true. They know that the air has also changed as much as the shape of the shores of Nope. In the times of our grandfathers, the waves which roll between these islands were always frozen over, from the hunting month to the month of the red singing bird. During the cold months, the canoe of the Indian hunter and fisherman was not permitted to traverse its dark and angry waters in quest of finny spoil, or in chase of the wild fowl. Then, to procure his food he took down his spear, and wandered far out on the frozen water to catch the foolish duck, which had suffered itself to be imbedded in the congealed clement; or, nearer to his cabin, he cut holes in the ice, and, as the stupid and benumbed fish glided across the opening, applied his unerring dart, and threw him to his delighted woman.

But the face of Nope changed, and with it the winters grew milder and milder. The hunting month was no longer the month of early snow, and when the red singing bird came, he hopped on an opening bud, and listened to the croaking of frogs. The alarm of the great sentinel [29] was heard no longer in the hour of darkness in the depth of the woods. There was too much sun for the hardy old warrior, and he followed his great chief, the brown eagle, to the regions of the north. Meantime the waters, no longer bound up with a chain by the Manitou of Cold, scooped out bays and heaped up headlands, till they made the shores of Nope crooked as the path of a bewildered white man, or the thread of a story which has no truth.

Once upon a time, in the month of bleak winds, a Pawkunnawkut Indian, who lived upon the main land, near the brook which was ploughed out by the great trout [30], was caught with his dog upon one of the pieces of floating ice, and carried in spite of his endeavours to Nope. Hitherto, it had remained unknown, and, as our people supposed, unapproachable. Several times they had attempted to visit it, but their canoes had always been swept away, or pushed back by some invisible hand, some friendly Manitou of the water, who feared danger to them, or some angry spirit of the island, who, by these signs, forbade their approach to his dominions. For many years, and ever since the memory of our fathers, the Indians, supposing it the residence of Hobbamock, the being who rules over evil men, sends disease and death to the Indians, breeds storms in the air, and utters the fearful sound in the black clouds, had carefully abstained from attempting to visit it. Nor was it altogether a mere uncertain dread of evil, which had operated on their minds to people it with living and moving beings. They could see at times men of monstrous stature moving rapidly over the island, and at all seasons in the calm evening, or when the winds blew from it, could hear sounds of anger or wailing, or of music and merriment, proceeding from its gloomy shades. And some pretended to have seen distinctly the form of a tall man wading into the water to grasp whales. The forced visit to its shores of Tackanash, the Pawkunnawkut, made them see it was not the dream of a sleeper who has eaten too much meat, but like that which men see with their eyes when they are awake, and would talk only what the Good Spirit may hear.

When Tackanash and his dog arrived at Nope, he found the man whose existence had been doubted by many of the Indians, and believed to have been only seen by deceived eyes, heard by foolish ears, and talked of by lying tongues, living in a deep cave near the end of the island, nearest the setting sun. And this was the account which Tackanash on his return gave the chiefs of the strange creature. He was taller than the tallest tree upon Nope, and as large around him as the spread of the tops of a vigorous pine, that has seen the years of a full grown warrior. His skin was very black; but his beard, which he had never plucked nor clipped, and the hair of his head, which had never been shaved, were of the colour of the feathers of the grey gull. His eyes were very white, and his teeth, which were only two in number, were green as the ooze raked up by the winds from the bottom of the sea. He was always goodnatured and cheerful, save when he could not get plenty of meat, or when he missed his usual supply of the Indian weed, and the strong drink which made him see whales chasing deer in the woods, and frogs digging *quawhogs*. His principal food was the meat of whales, which he caught by wading after them into the great sea, and tossing them out, as the Indian boys do black bugs from a puddle. He would, however, eat porpoises, when no larger fish were to be had, and even tortoises, and deer, and rabbits, rather than be hungry. The bones of the whales, and the coals of the fire in which he roasted them, are to be seen now at the place where he lived. I have not yet told my brothers the name of this big man of Nope—it was Moshup.

I hear the stranger ask, "Who was he?" I hear my brothers ask, "Was he a spirit from the shades of departed men, or did he come from the hills of the thunder? I answer, he was a Spirit, but whence he came, when first he landed in our Indian country, I know not. It was a long time ago, and the Island [31] was then very young, being just placed on the back of the Great Tortoise which now supports it. As it was very heavy the tortoise tried to roll it off, but the Great Spirit would not let him, and whipped him till he lay still. Moshup told the Pawkunnawkut that he once lived upon the main land. He said that much people grew up around him, men who lived by hunting and fishing, while their women planted the corn, and beans, and pumpkins. They had *powwows*, he said, who dressed themselves in a strange dress, muttered diabolical words, and frightened the Indians till they gave them half their wampum. Our fathers knew by this, that they were their ancestors, who were always led by the priests—the more fools they! Once upon a time, Moshup said, a great bird whose wings were the flight of an arrow wide, whose body was the length of ten Indian strides, and whose head when he stretched up his neck peered over the tall oak-woods, came to Moshup's neighbourhood. At first, he only carried away deer and mooses; at last, many children were missing. This continued for many moons. Nobody could catch him, nobody could kill him. The Indians feared him, and dared not go near him; he in his turn feared Moshup, and would seek the region of the clouds the moment he saw him coming. When he caught children, he would immediately fly to the island which lay towards the hot winds. Moshup, angry that he could not catch him, and fearing that, if the creature hatched others of equal appetite and ferocity, the race of

Indians would become extinct, one day waded into the water after him, and continued in pursuit till he had crossed to the island which sent the hot winds, and which is now called Nope. There, under a great tree, he found the bones of all the children which the great bird had carried away. A little further he found its nest, with seven hatched birds in it, which, together with the mother, he succeeded after a hard battle in killing. Extremely fatigued, he lay down to sleep, and dreamed that he must not quit the island again. When he waked, he wished much to smoke, but, on searching the island for tobacco, and finding none, he filled his pipe with *poke*, which our people sometimes use in the place of tobacco. Seated upon the high hills of Wabsquoy, he puffed the smoke from his pipe over the surface of the Great Lake, which soon grew dim and misty. This was the beginning of fog, which since, for the long space between the Frog-month and the Hunting-month, has at times obscured Nope and all the shores of the Indian people. This was the story which Moshup told Tackanash and his dog. If it is not true, I am not the liar."

Moshup, at the time when Nope was visited by Tackanash, had a wife of equal size with himself, and four sons, and a daughter, the former tall, strong, and swift, very expert at catching fish, and nimble in pursuit of deer, the latter beautiful, sweet-voiced, and bounding as the fawn. She would sit in the first of the evening, when the dew began to fall, and the shadows of men lengthened, and sing to her father songs of the land of the shades of evil men, songs which told of the crimes they had committed, and their repentance, and guilt, and compunction, and shame, and death. Though Moshup appeared to care little for any body, he nevertheless loved his little daughter, as he called her, whose head peered over the tallest trees, and whose voice was heard upon the main land. He shewed by many signs how much he loved his daughter. He strung up the teeth of the shark as a necklace for her, gathered the finest shells for her anklets, and always gave her the fattest slice of whale's meat to her portion.

The story of Tackanash, who very soon returned to Waquoit, and his description of the beauties of Nope, carried many of the Pawkunnawkuts thither to live. It was indeed a pleasant place, pleasant to the Indian, for it abounded with all the things he covets.

Its ponds were many, and stocked with fine fish and fat wild ducks; its woods were filled with deer, and the fertile banks of its streams overrun with wild vines, on which the grape thickly clustered, and where the walnut and the hazel-nut profusely loaded both bush and tree. Soon, the Pawkunnawkuts, at peace among themselves, and blessed by the Good Spirit with every thing they needed, became very numerous. There was not a pleasant spot on the island, from which did not arise the smoke of a cabin fire; nor a quiet lake, in which, in the months of flowers and fruits, you would not see Indian maidens laving their dusky limbs. The wild duck found no rest in his sunny slumber on the banks of Menemshe, the *pokeshawit* could no longer hide in the sedge, on the banks of his favourite Quampeche, and the deer, that went to quench his thirst in the Monnemoy, found the unerring arrow of the Indian in his heart.

But to Moshup the increase of the Indians seemed to give pain — none knew why, since the only enjoyments he appeared to covet were still as numerous as before. Whales were still plenty, *poke* was still plenty, and sleep and sunshine as easily enjoyed as ever. Though he never harmed the Indians, he grew discontented and unhappy, cross and peevish in his family, and sour and unneighbourly to all around him. He would beat his wife, if she did but so much as eat a falling scrap of the whale; toss his sons out of the cave, if, in the indulgence of boyish glee, they made the least noise while he was taking his nap; and box the ears of his little daughter, if she did but so much as look at an Indian youth.

Once upon a time, he bade his children go and play ball upon the beach that joins the hill [32] of White Paint to Nomensland, telling them that he would look on and see the sport. When they had played awhile, he made a mark with his great toe across the beach at each end, and so deep that the water followed the mark, leaving them surrounded with it, and in great danger of being drowned. When the tide at length began to flow across the beach, covering with water the whole space between the two high lands, the brothers took their little sister, and held her up out of the water, while Moshup, seated on the high cliffs, looked on. He told them to act as if they were going to kill whales, which they did, and were all turned into the fish called *killers*, a fish which has ever since been an enemy to whales, and is its greatest terror; As the sister was always a gay girl, painting her cheeks of many hues, and loving many-coloured ornaments, he commanded her to become, and she became, the striped killer. He bade her brothers be always very kind to her, and they have obeyed him.

When Moshup's wife learned the transformation of her children, she grieved very much for their loss. Night and day she did nothing hut weep and call for them, till, at length, Moshup grew tired of her noise, and, catching her up in his arms in a paroxysm of passion, he threw her as far as he could towards the country of the Narragansetts. She fell upon the point which juts far into the ocean, and over whose rocks the evil Manitou of the deep throws the great waves. The Indians call it Seconet. There, seated upon the rocks, she began to make all who came that way contribute to her support. She grew to be so cross and cruel, exacting so much from Indians, and making so much noise, that the Great Spirit changed her into a huge rock; the entire shape of which remained many years. But, when the Yengees came, some of them broke off her arms, fearing she would use them to their injury, and her head, lest she should plot mischief; but her body stands there now.

Moshup did not stay long on Nope after he had thrown away his wife, but while he did remain he was very good to the Indians, sending them many whales and other good things. He did very little save watch on the edge of the sea the sport of the killers, and in particular that which was striped, feeding it with certain pieces of fish, talking kindly to it, and always calling it by the name his daughter bore. Sometimes he would remain for many suns perched on the high cliff of White Paint, looking eagerly towards the place where he had thrown his old woman. At last, he went away, no one could say with certainty whither. Some of the Indians supposed they could see him at times walking on the high hills beyond the tides; others thought that he had gone back to his master; the Evil Spirit.

THE PHANTOM WOMAN.

A TRADITION OF THE WINNEBAGOES.

The days of Mishikinakwa, or the Little Turtle, were numbered, and the signs made visible of his approaching dissolution. There had been voices calling from the hills in the hour of the silent night, "Come, Mishikinakwa! she waits for thee." The *Nant-e-na*, or little spirits, which inhabit the earth, and the air, and the fire, and the water, according to their different natures, had all been busy, proclaiming the approaching translation of the chief from the troubles and hardships of this world to the happiness and quiet of another and a better. There were the rattling of their voices in the brook, and their whisperings in the air, and their hissings in the fire and their groanings in the earth. There were the falling of green leaves in the hour of calm, and the whirl of dry ones in the wind, the hoot of the grey owl on the ridge of his cabin, and the cry of the muckawiss in the hollow woods. The *Hottuk Ishtohoollo* or Holy People(1), with their relations the *Nana Ishtohoollo*, proclaimed from the clouds the threatened danger to the life of the warrior; while the *Nana Ookproose*, or accursed beings, howled out the tidings from their dwellings in the far west.

His years were not the years of an aged man; his hair was yet unstained by the frost of tune, his eye yet flashed with the fire of manhood, his step remained strong and steady. Yet, without hunger, without want, without pain, without disease, without a wound, in the prime of life, in the vigour of manhood, beloved by his friends, and feared by his enemies, the pride of the Winnebagoes was seen fast approaching the house of the dead.

None knew why, yet from one fatal day he was seen to droop, as a lily bends before, a fervid sun. From one fatal day his joy forsook him, and his eye became like a troubled water. His laugh had no more the joyousness of his healthful hour; his step was no more light and buoyant; food no more pleased his palate; sleep refreshed him no more. They came and sang the war-song at the door of his cabin, and he suffered them to depart without the answering shout. It was sung in his ears, "The Potowatomies are in in our war-path," but he raised not his head—"The Hurons have the scalp of thy brother's son," and no cry of vengeance burst from his lips. Slowly and gradually he faded away, and the time soon came that he could move no more from his bed of soft grass, but lay in silent expectation of the sound of the voice that calls the spirit home. It was while he was thus laid on the couch of death that he called the tribe around him, and told them why peace had departed from his soul, and why he waited anxiously the moment of his release from the chains of the flesh.

"I launched my canoe," said he, "upon the lake which has given its name to our nation, when the sun was getting low in the latter part of the month of the blooming lilies. Stilness was abroad upon the face of the waters, and the lake lay as calm as a babe rocked to sleep on the breast of its mother. Not the slightest ripple broke upon its surface, which was smooth as a field of ice frozen in a calm. Nothing marred its beauty, save now and then a sportive fish gliding over its bosom, or the swallow skimming along, catching the flies as they rose from the quenching of their thirst. The brown eagle was wheeling in spiral mazes towards his beloved sun, and I heard the chirping of the grasshopper, and the hum of the bee, each carolling away in his light-hearted labour. Afar lay the headlands, jutting into the lake, and the precipitous cliffs which rise over the deeper portion of its waters. Behind me were the smokes of the cabins of my people, and before me the beautiful expanse of the unruffled lake.

"As I brushed my light bark along, I saw, standing on the water at a distance from me, a very beautiful woman. My tongue has not the power to paint the charms of this stately and bright-eyed creature. She was tall, and as straight as a youthful fir, and her eyes shone with such brilliancy, that you could not endure to look upon them, any more than upon the sun, but turned away to contemplate other objects. She was clothed in a garment which glittered in the sun like the sparkling sand of the Spirits' Island [33], and her locks, which were yellow as the beams of that sun falling upon the folds of a cloud, flowed down her beautiful form till they swept the surface of the waters. Filled with sudden love for this beautiful creature, and anxious to secure her to myself, I spread the blanket of friendship to the wind [34], and paddled my canoe towards her. As I came near her, I could perceive a strange alteration in her appearance. Her shape gradually altered, her arms imperceptibly disappeared, her complexion assumed a different hue, her cheek no more glowed with life, her eyes had lost their brilliancy, her before glittering locks glittered no longer, and, when I came to the spot where she stood, I found only a shapeless monument of stone, having a human face and the fins and tail of a fish. For a long time I sat in amazement and uncertainly of purpose, fearing either to approach nearer, or to speak to the once loved, but now fearful object. At length, having made an offering of tobacco to propitiate the spirit, and deprecated its wrath for having dared to love it, I addressed it in these words:

"'Spirit, that wast beautiful but now, and hast only become divested of thy unequalled brilliancy because a poor mortal approaches thee! guardian spirit of our nation! messenger to myself from the Great Spirit! or whatever other name thou bearest, tell me why thou art changed. Why has thy form, but now straight as the fir and scarcely less tall, become crooked and misshapen, and no higher than the oak of two summers? why has thine eye, but now so bright that my own were pained by its brilliance, faded, and become of the lack-lustre colour of stone? And thy garments, which glittered like the folds of a cloud tinged by the beams of the setting sun — why have they partaken of the change? And thy locks, which were yellow and shining as the sparkling sand of the Spirits' Island, why have they become of the hue of the brown moth? Is it because I dared to think thee beautiful — because my heart dared to feel for thee the flame of sudden love! If thine anger hath been aroused at my presumption, forgive me, so thou wearest again the beautiful form that was thine when I first saw thee.'

"Having addressed the beautiful spirit thus, I paused for her reply. It came in tones soft and sweet as the wind of summer lightly sweeping the bosom of a prairie, and these were the words which belonged to them:

"'Mishikinakwa, it is not hatred of thee that makes me refuse to be seen by thee save at a distance, it is not hatred of thee which makes me refuse to re-animate that mass of stone and re-shape it to the proportions thou didst say were so beautiful. Oh no! I have seen thee before, chief of the Winnebagoes, and spirit as I am, have beheld thee with the eyes of love. But the beings which are not of clay are not allowed to associate with flesh and blood. I permitted thee a distant view of my face and form, that if thou thoughtest them worth the pains of death, thou mightst encounter those pains, and thy spirit, divested of its fleshly form, might fly to the arms of thy Light of the Shades, and rove with her through the valley of endless

bliss. Choose, then, between me, and a longer stay upon earth—
between the pains of a life which must be assailed by woes and
sorrows, by continual storm, angry winter, parching thirst, pinching
hunger, and chilling nakedness, and the joys which will attend thee
when thou art clasped in the arms of her thou lovest, and who will
return thy love with equal ardour. Unlike the maidens of the earth,
my charms can never fade; never, like theirs, can my love be turned
into hatred, or my heart grow cold, or my eyes cease to regard the
beloved object with favour. Loving on through all changes, and
loving on for ever, thy mind cannot fancy half the bliss which will
be thine—mine—ours—if thou darest to die.'

"She ceased speaking, but my pleased ears remained listening
long after her gentle voice had died away. And the delighted breeze
softly returned from the calm and transparent waters, and the spirit
of the echo gently repeated from the neighbouring hills, 'Unlike the
maidens of the earth, my charms can never fade; never like theirs
can my love be turned into hatred, or my heart grow cold, or my
eyes cease to regard the beloved object with favour. Loving on
through all changes, and loving on *for ever*, thy mind cannot fancy
half the bliss which will be thine—mine—ours—if thou darest to
die.

'Come to me, lover, come!
I'll wait thy death,
In the evening's breath,
On the brow of the mountain,
That shadows the fountain,
Come, my lover, come!

'Come to me, lover, come!
Again will I wear
Bright gold in my hair,
And my eyes shall be bright
As the beam of light.
Come, my lover, come!

'Come quick, my lover, come!
And thou shall be prest
To a faithful breast,

And thou shalt be led
To a bridal bed.
Mishikinakwa, come!'

"Thus called to the shades of happiness by so bright, and beautiful, and beloved, a being, how can I remain on the earth? Since that moment I have wished much to die; every day have I asked the Master of Life to take from me the breath he has given, and permit me to go to the land that holds the spirit of my affianced wife. I loathe the vile chain which binds me from her; I hate all the things I see, for they are all less beautiful than she; and all sounds pain mine ear, for is it not filled with her voice, a hundred times sweeter than aught ever heard on earth? Ha! her voice again! She calls me to her arms! She bids me come and drink of the crystal streams in the land of souls; she bids me come and chase with her the fawn and the kid, to bring her berries from the hills, and flowers from the vales, and to brush with our mingled footsteps, in early morning, the dew from the glades, and to blend in early evening the music of our lips, and the breath of our sighs, by the sides of the grass-wrapt fountain. She bids me come, and be clasped to a faithful breast, and called to a bridal bed. I come, beautiful spirit, to the appointed spot,

To the brow of the mountain,
That shadows the fountain.

Put then the bright gold in thy rolling locks, and let thine eyes shine as when I first saw thee. Be again as straight as the young fir, and array thyself in the garment which glittered like the sands of the Spirits' Island."

With a convulsive start, the warrior raised himself upon his couch to an upright posture. Gazing wildly around for a moment, he threw his arms forward, shouting "I come, beloved, I come!" and then falling back he lay a lifeless corpse. And so died Mishikinakwa, the Little Turtle of the Winnebagoes, of love for a phantom woman.

Note.

(1) *The Hottuk Ishtohoollo, or Holy People.*—p. 273.

Almost every hill and cavern has, in the eye of the Indian, its tutelary deity. The tradition entitled "The Mountain of Little Spirits" is one which paints a genuine belief.

Adair, in his History of the North American Indians, says, "They (viz. the Cherokees, Creeks, Choctaws, &c.) believe the higher regions to be inhabited by good spirits, whom they call *Hottuk Ishtohoollo*, and *Nana Ishtohoollo*, 'Holy People,' and relations to the 'Great Holy One?' The *Hottuk Ookproose*, or *Nana Ookproose*, 'accursed people,' or 'accursed beings,' they say possess the dark regions of the West; the former attend and favour the virtuous; and the latter in like manner accompany and have power over the vicious. Several warriors have told me," he says, "that their *Nana Ishtohoollo*, 'concomitant Holy Spirits,' or angels, have forewarned them, as by intuition, of a dangerous ambuscade, which must have been attended with certain death, when they were alone and seemingly out of danger; and, by virtue of the impulse, they immediately darted off, and with extreme difficulty escaped the crafty, pursuing enemy."

All the Northern Indians are very superstitious with respect to the existence of fairies. One of their tribes, the Chepewyans, speak of a race whom they call *Nant-e-na*, whom they say they frequently see, and who are supposed by them to inhabit the different elements of earth, sea, and air, according to their several qualities. To one or the other of these fairies they usually attribute any change in their circumstances either for better or worse; and, as they are led into this way of thinking entirely by the art of the conjurors, there is no such thing as any general mode of belief; for those jugglers differ so much from each other in their accounts of these beings, that those who believe any thing they say have little to do but change their opinions according to the will and caprice of the conjuror, who is almost daily relating some new whim or extraordinary event.

Every thing which is not easily understood is a spirit. Among the Creek Indians the Whip-poor-will is a spirit; the Jack o' Lantern is the same: and, with regard to the latter, they agree with the remnant of the Massachusett Indians, who believe it is the shape which the Evil Spirit takes in his visits to the sons of men. An old Indian woman, who lived some time as a domestic in my father's family, and was possessed of all the genuine traits of Indian character, was nearly thrown into convulsions by being caught a few rods from the house when one of these meteors made its appearance.

Tonti, in his account of De la Salle's Expedition, says: "They are so extravagant as to believe that every thing in the world has a spirit. It is upon this principle that are grounded all the foolish superstitions of their jugglers or Manitous, who are their priests or magicians."

THE TWO GHOSTS.

Once upon a time, many ages ago, there lived, near the shores of Lake Superior, a hunter, who was considered the most intrepid and expert in his vocation of all the hunters of the wilderness. His lodge, which was built with the steady reference to the wants of nature, which are always seen in the location of an Indian village or habitation, was situated in a remote part of the forest, at the distance of many days' journey from any other dwelling. Here, alone, and free from the bloody spirit of warfare which distinguished the men of his tribe, his days glided on like the quiet flow of a river that has no fall. He spent the period of light in the noble amusement of hunting, and his evenings in relating to his beautiful and bright-eyed wife the incidents which had befallen him that day in the chace; or he detailed those which had happened to him before she became the star of his lodge; or he spoke of their long-tried, and mutual love; or he fondly sketched scenes of future bliss; or he held on his knee, and pressed to his heart, the little pledge of their love, which now, for the first time, began to venture across the floor of his cabin without a hand to sustain it. As game was then very abundant, he seldom failed to bring home in the evening a store of meats sufficient to last them until the succeeding evening; and, while they were seated beside the pleasant fire of their lodge, partaking of the fruits of his labour, he would relate those tales, and enforce those precepts, which every good Indian thinks necessary for the instruction of his wife and children. This was his occupation, these were his pleasures. Who could ask a better or nobler than the first? who desire more intense, or purer, than the last? Far removed from all sources of disquiet, surrounded with all that they deemed necessary to their comfort, tenderly loving, and thence completely happy,

158

their lives passed away with scarcely less bliss than that of the disembodied spirits of the good in the Happy Shades. The breast of the hunter had never felt the pangs of remorse, for he had been a just man in all his dealings. He had never violated the laws of his tribe, by encroaching upon the hunting-grounds of his neighbours, or by taking that which did not of right belong to him. No offended hunter waylaid his steps to revenge an interference with his rights, no haughty chief came to the door of his lodge, to say, "Chippewa, give back that which you have stolen." No dream of the fame to be acquired by war — by the frequent slaughter of unoffending women and children, or even of hardy warriors, his equals in strength and valour — danced before his eyes, filling his sleep with bloody images and sights of horror. The white man had not yet come to fill the mind of the poor Indian with cravings for things which were not needed till they were known; as yet, he had not been taught that clothes and blankets were necessary to his comfort, or that game could not be killed without guns. The skin of the buffalo, the moose, the bear, and the deer, answered the purpose of protecting him from the heat and the cold; and the bow and arrow well supplied the place of the gun, especially when pointed by the steady hand and unerring eye of an Indian hunter. Having then, no more than now, occasion to fell large trees, the axes of stone in use among us when white men landed on our shores answered all the simple purposes of Indian life. Iron and powder, which, with *one* other fatal gift, have already led to the almost total, and will soon effect the total, extinction of the race by furnishing us with a surer mode of destruction, had not yet found their way into those remote and peaceful forests, nor had the white man poured that one other fatal gift, his wrathful phial of liquid fire [35] upon our devoted Indian race. Our wants were then few, easily supplied, and totally independent of white men.

Peacefully glided away the life of the Chippewa hunter, happy in his ignorance, but still happier in his simplicity. Relying fully upon the superintending care of an overruling Great Spirit, whom he had always served, no anxious dread of present want, no fears for the future filled his bosom. His life was as unruffled as the surface of a lake in the calm of the summer.

One evening, during the winter season, when snow covered the earth, and ice locked up the waters of the Great Lake, it chanced that this happy Chippewa hunter remained out much later than usual. His wife sate lonesome in her tent, and began to be agitated with fears that some fatal accident had befallen him. Darkness had already veiled the face of nature, and gathering gloom rested upon the brow of night. She listened attentively, to catch the sounds of coming footsteps, but nothing could be heard but the wind whistling around the sides of their slender lodge, and through the creaking branches of the surrounding forest of oaks and pines. Time passed away in this state of suspense; he came not, and every moment augmented her fears, and added to the loneliness of her heart. With the little pledge of their mutual love clasped to her bosom, she sat counting every moment as it flew, with difficulty commanding her tears, and singing them down with fragments of some of the simple songs which all the sons of the earth are in the habit of using, to while away hours rendered weary by any passing occurrence. At length her heart gave way, and she burst into a deep and fervent passion of tears. Suddenly she heard the sound of approaching footsteps upon the frozen surface of snow. Not doubting that it must be her beloved husband, she quickly undid the loop, which held, by an inner fastening, the door of the lodge, and, throwing it open, beheld two strange females standing in front of it. She could not hesitate what course to pursue. She bade them enter and warm themselves, knowing, from the distance to the nearest cabin, that they must have walked a long way. When they had entered she invited them to remain. She soon observed that they were total strangers in that part of the country, and the more closely she scrutinized their manners, their dress, and their dignified deportment, the stronger grew her conviction that they were persons of no ordinary character. No efforts, no persuasions, could induce them to come near the fire; they took their seats in a remote part of the lodge, and drew their garments about their persons in such a manner as almost completely to hide their faces. They seemed shy and taciturn, spoke not, and remained as motionless as stones fixed in the earth. Occasionally, though but seldom, glimpses could be caught of their faces, which were pale and ghastly, even to the hue of death. Their eyes she saw were vivid but sunken, their cheekbones as prominent as if all flesh had left them, and their whole persons, as far as could be judged, emaciated and fleshless. Seeing that her strange guests, of whom she now began to feel much fear, avoided all conversation, and appeared anxious to escape observation, she forbore to question them, and sat in silence until her husband entered. He had been led farther than usual in pursuit of game, but returned with the carcase of a large and very fat deer. No sooner had he laid his spoil on the floor of his cabin, than the mysterious females, exclaiming, "Behold! what a fine, fat animal!" immediately ran up, and pulled off pieces of the whitest fat, which they ate with great avidity. As this is esteemed the choicest part of the animal, and is generally, by Indian courtesy, left to the share of the master of the lodge, such conduct appeared very strange to the hunter. Supposing, however, that they had been a long time without food, for he attributed their extreme leanness and ghastliness to hunger and privation, he forbore to accuse them of rudeness, and his wife, following her husband's example, was equally guarded in her language. On the following evening, the same scene was repeated. He brought home the best portions of the deer he had killed, and, while in the act of laying it down before his wife, according to custom, the two females again ran up, and tore off, as on the first night, the choicest and most delicate portions, which they ate with the same eagerness and unappeasable avidity as before. Such unhandsome behaviour, such repeated abuses of his hospitality, were calculated to raise displeasure on the brow of the hunter, but still the deference due to strange guests induced him to pass it over in silence. Observing their partiality for this part of the animal, he resolved the next day to anticipate their wants, by cutting off and tying up a portion of the fat for each. These parcels he placed upon the top of his burthen, and, as soon as he entered the lodge, he gave to each her portion. Still the guests appeared dissatisfied, and took more from the carcass lying before the wife. Many persons would have repressed this forwardness, by some look, word, or action, but this man, being a just and prudent man, slow to provocation, and patient under afflictions of every kind, abstained from any of them. He was, perhaps, the more disposed to this quiet spirit of forbearance, from a suspicion that his guests were persons of distinguished rank, who chose thus to visit him in disguise, and also from reflecting, that the best luck had attended him in hunting, since the residence of the mysterious strangers beneath his roof.

In other respects, the deportment of the females was unexceptionable, though marked with some peculiarities. They were quiet, modest, and discreet. They maintained a cautious silence through the day, neither uttering a word nor moving, but folded up in their skin mantles they remained in the corner of their lodge. When it became dark, they would get up, and, taking those instruments which were then used in breaking up and preparing fuel, would repair to the forest. There they would busy themselves in seeking dry limbs and fragments of trees, blown down by tempests. When a sufficient quantity had been gathered to last till the succeeding night, they carried it home upon their shoulders; then, carefully putting every thing in its proper place within the lodge, they resumed their seats and their studied silence. They were ever careful to return from their nocturnal labours before the dawning of day, and were never known to go out before the hour of dusk. In this manner they repaid, in some measure, the kindness of the hunter, and relieved his wife from her most laborious duties.

Thus nearly the whole winter passed away, every day leading to some new development of character or office of friendship, which served to endear the parties to each other. Their faces daily lost something of that deathlike hue which had at first marked them, and they visibly improved in strength. They began to throw off some of that cold reserve and forbidding austerity, which had kept the hunter so long in ignorance of their true character. Every day, their appearance and behaviour approximated more nearly to that of the beings of ordinary life. One evening the hunter returned very late, after having spent the day in toilsome exertion. Again he deposited the product of his hunt at the feet of his wife, and again the silent females began to tear off the flesh as before, though with still greater rudeness and ill-breeding. The patience of the wife was completely lost, she could no longer controul her feelings, and suffered the thought to pass her mind, "Their conduct is certainly very strange! how can I bear with it any longer!" She did not, however, give utterance to her feelings in words. But an immediate change was seen in the females. They became unusually reserved, and gave evident signs of being uneasy in their situation. The good hunter immediately perceived this change, and, fearful that they had taken offence, so soon as they had retired to rest, he enquired of his wife whether any harsh expression had escaped her lips during the day. She replied that she had uttered nothing to give the least offence. He now tried to compose himself to sleep, but he felt restless and uneasy, for he could plainly hear the sighs and half-smothered lamentations of the two females. Every moment added to his conviction that his guests had taken deep offence, and, as he could not banish this idea from his mind, he raised himself on his couch, and addressed the sobbing inmates thus:

"Tell me, ye women that have so long been the inmates of my lodge, what is it that causes you pain of mind, and makes you unceasingly utter these sighs? Has the wife of my bosom given you any cause of offence while I was absent in the chase? My fears persuade me that, in some unguarded moment, she has forgotten what is due to the rights of hospitality, and used expressions ill befitting the mysterious character which you seem to sustain. Tell me, ye strangers from a strange country — ye women who appear to be not of this world — what is it that causes you pain of mind, and makes you utter these unceasing sighs?"

"It is not for this that we weep; it is not for this that we sigh," replied the mysterious women. "No unkind expressions have been used towards us since our residence in your hospitable lodge. We have received from you all the affectionate attentions which we could expect, far more than could reasonably be asked of one who procures his food and supports his family by a life of incessant toil and labour. We thank you for all your kindness. No, it is not for this: it is not for ourselves that we weep. We are weeping for the fate of mankind. We are weeping for the fate of mortals whom death awaits at every stage of their existence — weak mortals! whom death cuts down equally while the bloom of youth is on their cheek, and when their hair is whitened by the frosts of time — proud, vain men! whom hunger pinches, cold benumbs, and poverty emaciates — frail beings! who are born in tears, who are nurtured in tears, who die in tears, and whose whole course is marked upon the thirsty sands of life in a broad line of tears. It is for these that we weep.

"You have spoken truly, brother; we are not of this world. We are Spirits from the land of the dead, sent upon the earth to try the sincerity of the living. It is not for the dead but the living that we mourn. It is not for the dead, whose flesh quietly reposes in the dust, and whose souls repair to the mansions of happiness, that we mourn, but for the living who are subjected to many, many pains, and beset with innumerable troubles and anxieties. It was by no means necessary that your wife should express her thoughts by words; we knew them ere they were spoken. We saw that for once displeasure towards us had arisen in her heart. It is enough—our mission is ended. We came hither but to try you. We knew before we came that you were a kind husband, an affectionate father, a temperate and honest man. We saw, from the mansions of the blest, the patience with which you bore your disappointments in the chace; the gratitude to the Great Spirit which you always evinced; the tribute to his goodness which you always paid when your hunts were successful, and you were enabled to return to your cabin with the wealth of the forest. Still we find that you have some of the weaknesses of a mortal, and your wife is found still more wanting in our eyes. But it is not for you alone that we weep; it is for the fate of mankind.

"Often, very often, has the widowed husband exclaimed, 'Oh death, how cruel, how relentless thou art, to take from me my best friend, my beloved wife, in the spring of her youth, in the prime of her strength, in the morning of her usefulness, in the bloom of her beauty! Just when I had come to know her best, and to love her most, thou didst take her from my arms, leaving me to pine in unavailing regrets. If thou wilt permit her, just Judge! to return once more to my arms, and again be the star of my humble abode, my gratitude shall never cease; my thankfulness shall be daily manifested in songs and sacrifices to thy name. The high hill shall hear the cry of a man with clay in his hair, and the valley shall be filled with the smoke of a sacrificial flame. I will raise my voice continually to thank the Master of Life for the return to my arms of his excellent gift. And to her shall the return be productive of unbounded felicity. I will devote my time to study how I can best promote her happiness, while she is permitted to remain, and our lives shall roll away, like a pleasant stream through a vale of flowers.' If a parent has been bereaved of a child rendered dear by its innocence and sportive fondness, he has said, while tears were furrowing his cheek, 'Great Manitou, wilt thou return this beloved child for a few more years to my bosom? It was but young and little. Its voice, softer than the breath of spring, had not fashioned its tones of tenderness into words. I had not heard it thank me for the gift of life; it was a flower blasted in the bud. If thou wilt permit its return, it shall be taught to sing thy praises; it shall be made to walk in the straight path; it shall be a just hunter and a true warrior.' The bereft lover has besought the Great Spirit for the return of his deceased mistress: his petition has painted the charms of her voice sweet as the south wind; her step light and graceful as the fawn's; her locks clustering like grapes. And, 'Oh!' he has said, 'will it disarrange the harmony of thy system, if she may but for a little while return to my arms; if but for a few, a very few years, she may illumine the darkness of my lodge by the splendour of her eyes, and send joy to my soul by the soft tones of her voice, and the sound of her steps?' Thus, also, has the mother prayed for her daughter; the wife for her husband; the sister for her brother; the friend for his bosom-companion, until the sounds of mourning, and the cries of the living, have pierced the very recesses of the dead. Among those who have wished their departed friends to return, were many who were cruel and unkind to them while living. These have not failed to promise the most endearing conduct, should their relatives be allowed to return.

"The Great Spirit has, at length, consented to make a trial of their sincerity, by sending us upon the earth at a very severe season of the year, and in a time of general scarcity. He did this to see how we should be received, coming as strangers, no one knowing whence. It was necessary that this severity of proof should be exacted. Three months were allowed us to make the trial; and if, during that time, no irksomeness of feeling had been evinced, no angry passions excited, at the place where we should have taken up our abode, all those in the land of spirits, whom their relations had desired to return, would have been restored to them. We had already passed more than half the time assigned to us, and had already dared to hope for a successful termination of our mission. Had your wife maintained those feelings of unmixed generosity and kindness which have heretofore marked her conduct, the ransom would have been complete. When the leaves began to bud, and the birds to sing their sweet songs of love, and to warble their gentle burdens of gratitude for the return of their beloved spring, our mission would have been successfully terminated. The deceased husband and wife would then have been each returned to the arms of his or her rejoicing partner, the maiden to the arms of her tender lover, the infant to the bosom of its adoring mother. But it is now too late. Our trial is finished, and we are called to the pleasant fields, and beautiful shades, whence we came. It is not for those who remain in those shades; it is not for the souls we left in the abode of happy spirits, that we grieve, but for you that are left on earth.

"Brothers, it is necessary and proper, that one man should die to make room for another who is born in his place; otherwise the world would be filled to overflowing. It is just, that the goods gathered by one should be left to be divided by others, for in the land of spirits there is no want. There is neither sorrow nor hunger, death nor pain, in that land. Pleasant fields filled with game lie spread before the eye, and birds of most beautiful plumage and shapes are singing on every bush. Every stream is filled with fat fish, and every hill is crowned with groves of trees, whose fruit is sweet and pleasant to the taste and beautiful to the eye. No piercing winds rack the bones, no storms, no whirlwinds, assail the ear. All kinds of games have been invented to amuse, and many, very many, instruments to play upon. It is not here, brother, but *there*, that men begin truly to live. It is not for those that rejoice through those pleasant groves, but for you that are left behind, that we weep.

"Brother, take our thanks for your hospitality. Regret not our departure. We go not in anger with thee, nor with thy wife. Fear not evil. Thy luck shall still be good in the chace, and a bright sky prevail over thy lodge. Mourn not for us, for no corn will spring up from tears; but join us in lamentations for the fate of mankind. Mourn for mortals whom death awaits at every stage of their existence; whom death cuts down equally while the bloom of youth is on their cheek, and when their hair is whitened by the frosts of time—proud, vain men, whom hunger pinches, cold benumbs, and poverty emaciates—frail beings, who are born in tears, nurtured in tears, die in tears, and whose whole course is marked upon the thirsty sands of life by a broad line of tears. It is for those that we weep."

The spirits ceased; but the hunter had no power over his voice to reply. As they continued their address, he saw a light beaming from their faces, and gradually a blue vapour filling the whole lodge with an unnatural light. As soon as the females ceased speaking, a deep and dense darkness prevailed. He listened, but the sobs of the spirits had ceased. He heard the door of his tent open and shut, but he never saw more of his mysterious visitors. Their promise was not forgotten; he found the success which they spoke of. He became a most celebrated hunter, and never wanted for any thing necessary to his ease. He became the father of many children, all of whom grew up to manhood: and health, peace, and long life, were the rewards of his hospitality.

THE VISION OF THE ABNAKIS CHIEF.

Wangewaha, the great chief of the Abnakis, in one of his hunting excursions, lay down beneath the shade of a stately fir, on the shore of the stormy lake, beside which he was born, and the spirit of sleep came over him. He dreamed a dream, the like of which was never dreamed before among the red men of the forest. That dream hath come to pass; each jot and tittle of it has been performed; the things were done before mine own eyes, and the words spoken into mine own ears. Listen to the dream of Wangewaha, the great war chief of the Abnakis.

He saw, far in the east, upon the face of the waters, a white cloud which seemed to be impelled by a strong wind, and it was approaching the shores of the same land in which the Abnakis dwelt. Along its lower extremity appeared a narrow outline of exceeding blackness, and ever and anon the cloud became larger or grew less, now increased and now diminished, as the wind, or other causes, spread it out, or contracted it. At length, the wind, which before blew towards the land, veered and blew from it, but, strange to tell, the cloud was not carried back, but kept its course onward in defiance of the wind, and thus fared the cloud.

Upon the shore, watching with extreme and undivided interest the progress of the cloud, stood many of the sons of the forest. Wonder and astonishment had seized their souls, at the strange and hitherto unheard-of sight of a low, compact, dark cloud, moving rapidly against a strong wind. They saw that it was of unusual shape, and that there were other circumstances connected with it, such as are not usual with the spirit-mists of the air. Rightly deeming it a cloud from some very far region, perhaps some aërial messenger sent by the Great Spirit to communicate an important errand, they awaited in silent awe the progress of that to which they could not give a name. Yet, deeming it possible that grim war might in some one of his thousand forms be hidden under the semblance of a cloud—that hostile beings might inhabit what appeared but thin air—they prepared to oppose violence with violence, and to meet battle with manful battle. Some went and cut new lance poles, others tough and elastic bows. The priests prepared sacrifices to appease the spirit, if spirit it were, and sang propitiatory songs, in which they first called it a good Spirit, and thanked it as such for the fat deer and mooses it had sent to their hunting-grounds, and the juicy fish which filled their waters, and the tender fowls which stocked their lakes. Then they addressed it as the Spirit of Evil, deprecating its wrath, and imploring its mercy, beseeching it, if it came in anger, to go away and discharge its venom elsewhere; if it came to bring them rich gifts, to be speedy about it, for such never came too soon.

In the mean time, the cloud came every moment nearer, till, at last, it was scarcely the flight of an arrow distant from the shore. Then gradually it disappeared, and, in its stead, appeared a large animal, with innumerable arms and legs of all sizes and shapes, and of all lengths, and of several colours. Perched on various parts of the legs and arms of this strange animal were other animals, whose appearance was unlike any other being ever beheld by the Indians. They wore in some respects the character of man—were gifted with his strength and wisdom, his power and capacities—were by turns a prey to lust, ambition, hate, despair, revenge—commencing life with tears, and dying with a sigh. Their fangs were for venom the fangs of a snake; their cunning, the cunning of a fox; and their fierceness, the fierceness of a mountain cat, or a panther. Very nimble they seemed, and sprang about the legs and arms of the bigger animal, like a squirrel leaping from one branch of a tree to another branch. One ran up a rope till it had reached one of the arms; another slid down in like manner; a third was perched half-way up; a fourth was running to and fro on the back of the animal. At length, one of the little animals dropped a great rope, to which was appended an enormous forked tree, and this operated to tie up the bigger animal, which rolled about very much, as if in vain attempts to liberate itself from the thraldom to which they had subjected it.

After a while, there was a smaller animal seen leaving the side of the bigger, as a kid leaves the side of its mother, similar in shape to the bigger, but having neither arms nor legs; and, upon the back of this animal, many of the smaller animals sought the shore. When they had arrived, they presented themselves to the eyes of the astonished Abnakis, in a shape which seemed to the sleeper to be that of a panther, wearing the shape of man, yet fierce and cruel as any ever found in the wilds of the river of the Abnakis. With this fierce and cruel disposition was coupled a cunning beyond that of the fox, and a malignity greater than the rattlesnake's. Their fierceness and cruelty, and the malignity and savage ferocity of their natures, were hidden, however, under a show of peace. They laughed, and grinned, and did the other things, which mortals do when they are, or pretend to be, pleased, making the unsuspecting Abnakis think that they were their very good friends, when they were only waiting for a chance to rend them limb from limb. Nor was their disposition wholly hidden by the mask, which these worthless and wicked beasts had only assumed for the purpose of beguiling the poor red man. Occasionally the panther would show his teeth, and the rattlesnake his malignity, though the cunning of the fox would soon throw a veil over the one, and hush the noise of the other.

Strange, indeed were the bodies, tempers, and dispositions of the beasts, which thus passed in sleep before the eyes of the dreaming chief. He saw them invested with the habits and feelings of men, as they appeared to be gifted with their capacities and acquirements. They had courage, not indeed as the Abnakis have it, not the courage which delights in the post of danger, and encounters difficulties for the mere honour of overcoming them, but in another, and less active form, that of endurance. And their wisdom and power were greater than the wisdom and power of the Abnakis priests, who could draw water from the clouds, and foretell the coming of tempests and storms(1). The wisdom and power of the strange beasts was very great—they were subtler than the fox or the beaver, and stronger than the bear.

Among these beasts, there was one of most transcendent beauty, who appeared to be their queen. She bore the form of a stately woman. She was clothed, not as beasts generally are, in fur, but in a robe of an unknown material, that reached to her feet, which were shrouded in a veil of so thin a texture, that the pure flesh was transparent through them, and not shod with mocassins, but with something of a different form. Around her head was bound a grape-vine, from which hung beautiful clusters of rich, ripe grapes, intermingled with locks of hair, of a hue resembling the yellow leaf. Her round and plump arms were bound with bracelets of a very bright material; and, upon her long and slender fingers, were rings set with sparkling stones, of various and exceedingly radiant hues— green, blue, purple, white. In one of her delicate hands, she carried a small bunch of grain, of a kind which was never seen before by the Abnakis, but the ears of which bent over like the wings of a hawk hovering over his prey, or or a bird settling upon its perch. The same fair hand carried the instrument wherewith it was reaped. The other hand bore a huge shell and a three-forked sceptre, emblems of her dominion upon the element, which supported the cloud upon which she came. Upon her breast she wore a shield, on which was painted the likeness of two animals, one of them wearing a shaggy mane, and both looking exceedingly fierce and warlike. There were upon this shield other paintings and devices, which even the ingenuity of the priests could not explain. Altogether, the appearance of the being, animal, or whatever it was, which the Abnakis dreamer saw, was exceedingly noble and beautiful. They who came with her said she was the genius of the land beyond the Great Water, the guardian spirit of an island more powerful than all the world besides. And surely great power was written in her countenance, and authoritative command engraved on the lines of her face.

Then Wangewaha saw, and a being also wearing the appearance of a woman came down from the shades, and confronted the stranger. She was of a still taller stature than the other, and of the same complexion as the inhabitants of the land, her skin red, black her hair, her eyes shining, her step yet more noble and commanding, and her bearing prouder and more haughty than that of her who appeared to be her younger sister. Her hair, long, straight, and black, hung over her shoulders till it reached her feet; her mocassins were of the gaudiest colours; and beads, and shells, and wampum, were profusely employed in adorning her person. Above her head towered feathers, the canieu's or war-eagle's, and the painted vulture's—in her hands she carried a spear and a sheaf of arrows. A bow hung at one of her shoulders, while over the other was carelessly thrown the game slain by her archery. Her robe was made of the furs of the gayest forest animals, and her emblems were an ear of maize and the antlers of a buck. Stately she moved, as a wild swan on a calm lake, or a black cloud over the brow of a mountain; and the boldness of her demeanour, and the fierceness of her eyes, contrasted strongly with the softness and effeminacy of her that seemed her younger, and more delicate, sister.

Anon, these two sisters entered into speech with each other, and the artless and unsuspecting soul of the one was contrasted strongly with the cunning of the other. Said the stranger to her who was of the land, "Thou hast a most beautiful land."

"It is indeed a most beautiful land," answered the other.

"It has lofty mountains."

"Its mountains are very lofty."

"It has many beautiful and rapid rivers."

"It has."

"Its suns—"

"Are bright as the eyes of a dove."

"Its winds—"

"Soft as the breath of a young maiden."

"Methinks I should like to live in thy cabin—to rove uncontrolled through thy green glades, and to listen in dreamy and indolent repose to the merry music of thy waterfalls."

"Do, and thou shalt be welcome," replied the dark but beautiful, the stern but guileless, genius of the land.

"Knowest thou not that we are sisters?" asked the bright-eyed, fair-skinned, stranger.

"Nay, I knew it not," replied she of the wilderness.

"We are, and we have two others—thou, the youngest, and I thy next elder. I am come hither to direct thy footsteps, and to render thee my assistance in beautifying the clime so beautiful in itself, and to give to those over whom thou presidest the light of the knowledge I have conducted to my own realms. I have brought with me those who are the pioneers of my footsteps whithersoever I go."

"It is well," answered the genius of the wilderness. "Take as much as thou wilt of my lands. Choose for thyself the fairest spots—make my people as thine own—we are sisters, thou sayest, and I believe thee, for I love thee—sisters should dwell together in peace and love. Yon river bank is very fertile."

"It is indeed very fertile," answered the strange genius, her countenance brightening up as she surveyed the beautiful spot to which her attention was directed.

"Thou shalt have it for thine own," said the elder sister kindly.

"Thou art very good," answered the other. "What use dost thou make of yonder broad, and beautiful, and rapid river?"

"It furnishes food to my people. In the summer moons, the light canoes of my beloved red men are seen gliding over it in swift pursuit of the sturgeon; the fishes which sport in its clear bosom are the sweetest in all the waters of my wide domain."

"I should like to have that river to be mine own," said the pale genius.

"I can spare it," answered the other kindly. "It is thine."

"Yon is a beautiful lake," said the younger. "How calm and unruffled is its surface!"

"It is a very beautiful lake, but thou hast not seen it in its most beautiful season," answered the elder. "Thou shouldst behold it when it waves a wide sea of water-lilies, white as the snow of winter, or when myriads of gay wild-fowl skim its level surface, or settle down upon its pellucid bosom, to take their repast. Then it is indeed beautiful—very beautiful."

"A river and a lake should go together," said the younger.

"They should," answered she of the land, "nor will I be the one to separate them. I give thee the lake."

"How much loftier than all the mountains of my own clime is that which I see towering in the distance towards the land of the warm breezes!"

"That mountain is indeed very lofty," answered the dark Genius.

"I have a noble river, with a flowery bank rising above it, and I have a level lake, but thou hast not given me a mountain, to whose cool and refreshing breezes I may retire, when the fervid and scorching suns of summer invade the lowlands. I would—thou wilt deem me greedy as the hawk or the heron—I would have some such spot, whose breezes, when they kindly dispense health, nerve the soul to great actions, and within whose wild and inaccessible fastnesses, which, ever since Time was, have been the keepers of the free, the weak may find a resting-place, and the wearied by oppression a refuge."

"Take thou the mountain, and name what else thou wilt have."

"Only a few more rivers and a few more vales, which thou canst easily spare, and another mountain for a further refuge, and some more lakes to breed more wild-fowl in, and a forest or two well stocked with deer, and a part of the Great Lake to put my whales in—nothing more, except it be another vale, and another mountain, and another river, and a piece more of the sea."

The dark Genius of the land smiled at the *narrow* wishes of her younger sister, and replied, that she could spare them all. So the younger sister appropriated to herself the highest mountains, and the most pleasant vales, and the broadest lakes, and the most rapid rivers, and a large piece of the sea to put whales in, and some forests well stocked with deer, and said, "she had taken so little it was scarcely worth thanking for."

Then the dreamer saw in his sleep that, at her bidding, the strange beasts which came in the cloud issued forth to take possession. How their eyes gloated upon the fair gifts which had been made them by the kind spirit of the land! And how grateful they appeared to be, and how exceedingly kind and affectionate they were to the poor Indians! They stroked their heads gently with one hand, while with the other they released them from their oppressive burdens—their beaver skins and their maize—indeed they were too kind. Then to gratify them still further, they produced a burning water [36], which they distributed among them, assuring them of its power to create pleasing images in the mind, and to make bright visions dance before the eyes of those who drank it. The Indians drank as they were bidden, and realised the predicted effects. What a wonderful medicine was the strong water! Under its potent influence, the mirror of the soul became enlarged, and a thousand images, till then unseen, floated before the mental eye. Then might a man receive certain intimations of the object he should choose as his protecting spirit, and astonish his brothers by a medicine of strange proportions and great power. And secrets of the land of souls—the way to pass the "narrow bridge over the fearful river," and how to stay the anger of the dog that guards it at the point where the Huron passes—how to tread the sharp and steep rock upon which the Chippewa finds entrance to his land of rest—all this, and much more, to be attained by no other means, was learned from the strong waters given to the Abnakis by the strange spirit. And Wangewaha, the dreamer, woke from his sleep, rubbed his eyes, and indulged in deep thought of what the dream might portend.

Again he sunk to sleep, and again he dreamed. Still his dream was of strange creatures, aliens to his land, and usurpers of the rights of its native sons. But they had multiplied till their numbers were as the sands upon the sea shore. He stood in imagination upon a lofty hill, and cast his eyes upon the broad lands beneath him. How changed! The forests had been swept away, the land was cleared of its mossy old oaks, and lofty pines, and cedars, but, where they once raised their leafy heads to the winds of heaven, now rose cabins, white as the folds of a cloud, and glittering in the sun like a sheet of ice in a winter's day. The broad and rapid river, as well as the waters of the Great Lake, was marked in streaks of white foam by the many clouds traversing it, like that he had seen in his first dream. The lofty mountains were seamed like the breast of a tattooed warrior(2), by the roads which the strangers had made over it. The vales waved with the yellow wheat, and, herds of tame bisons lay resting on the grassy knolls, or stood grouped at the outlets of the fields, which the industrious strangers had girded in with fences of rock.

And what had become of the former inhabitants of the soil? where were the dusky men who met the strange creatures upon the shore, and bade them welcome, and gave them the fat things of the sea and the land for their subsistence, and warm furs to protect them from the searching winds of the Snow-Moon, and taught them how to follow the trail of forest animals, and to thread, unerringly, their way for many successive nights through the lonely wilderness, by the flow of streams and the course of fishes, and the light of the Hunter's Star, and the moss upon the oaks, and the flight of birds? Listen, and I will tell you.

He sees upon the edge of a stream, overgrown with a thick grove of alders and luxuriant vines, an Indian man and woman. The woman held in her arms a dying child—at the feet of the man, lay a lean and famished dog. Deep thought was in the eye of the one, and absorbing grief in that of the other. Now the hunter cast his eyes into the depths of the river in anxious search for the signs of the approach of the finny people; now he laid his ear to the earth after the manner of his race, when they would detect the sound of footsteps.

"Didst thou see aught in the current, which thine eye is searching?" asked the wife tremulously, fixing her bright black eye, moistened with a tear, upon her hungry infant.

"I saw nothing in the current," answered the hunter. "The net of the stranger hath swept from the flood that which was in part the food of our tribes, when he first became acquainted with these shores. The barbed spear no more brings up the sleeping conger; the Indian throws his hook into the once populous stream, but it returns with the bait untouched."

"Did thy quick ear catch the sound of aught in the mazes of the wood?" asked the fond mother, and her tears fell thick on the cheeks of her little babe.

"My ear caught no sound in the mazes of the wood," answered the hunter. "How should it? The stranger hath left nothing save the mouse, and the mole, and few of them. He has swept away the beloved retreats of the bounding beauty of the forest, the nimble deer, and none are left in the glades, where once they were thicker than the stars. The bear, and the wolf, and the panther, love not their crafty brother, and have gone yet deeper into the forest. The wild duck feeds now in the deep waters only, the mother teaches her brood that death lurks behind the wood-skirted shore."

"Then must this little child—thine and mine—our first-born, die of hunger. Yet bethink thee. I see among yonder lofty trees a cabin, the whiteness of which tells us that one of the despoilers of our joys hath there taken up his abode."

"Wouldst thou have the son of Alknomook—the son of the rightful lord—himself the rightful lord of these wide regions—beg bread from the stranger?"

"Not to save thy life or mine would I ask it, but what would I not do to save the life of this beautiful babe, which the Great Spirit granted to my prayers, when for sixty moons I had lived in thy cabin a disgraced woman(3)."

"Not therefore should the soul of an Indian warrior bend to a master. I cannot beg."

"What was the dream which thou hadst in the last Worm-Moon?"

"Thou sayest well—it was of vengeance had by means of the boy. The son of Alknomook will humble his pride—he will wipe off the war paint, which he laid as deep on his face as the memory of his wrongs weigh on his heart, and he will supplicate the stranger to give him food for his little one."

Still the sleeping chief continued to take note of the things which occurred. He beheld the enfeebled and emaciated Indians at the dwelling of the proud stranger. The stranger sat at the door of his lofty cabin, and thus he addressed the friendless outcasts:

"Why have you dared to trespass on my soil, to bruise my pretty flowers with your rude feet, and to frighten my flocks and herds with your shrill halloos?"

The son of the forest was about to reply fiercely, when his ear caught the plaintive moan of his famished child, and he controlled the tempest of wrath which was rising in his bosom.

"Thine eyes are the eyes of an owl by daylight," replied he calmly. "They have seen a thing which has not happened. The son of Alknomook did not bruise the flowers of the pale face, nor frighten his flocks and herds by his shrill halloos. Wilt thou give me a morsel of food for my famished child?"

"Begone, thou Indian dog!" said the proud and cruel man. "Thou shalt have no food here."

"But my child will die of hunger."

"If thy child die of hunger, there will be a red skin less. Back to thy woods, and herd with wolves and panthers, thy fit associates."

The soul of the stern but generous warrior filled with ire and the spirit of vengeance, as he poured out his feelings in the emphatic language of his people. "Not so spoke the Abnakis to the weary, naked, and hungry, men who came to their shores, and besought them to grant them shelter," said he. "We gave them the food from our own mouths, and took the skins which fenced our wigwams to protect them from the winds of the cold moon." Nor did he cease speaking till he had denounced upon the pale faces the wrath of the Great Spirit for the injuries they had inflicted upon the Indians.

Ah, what is that which draws tears to the eyes of the dreamer, and brings sighs to his labouring heart? He beholds an Indian mother lying dead in the skirts of the forest. Upon her arm is laid a little child, and beside them, leaning on a bow, is the husband of the one and the father of the other. Sorrow has bowed him down, as far as the soul of an Indian may be bowed—there are no tears in his eyes, yet distress is written on the features of his face, in letters of enduring agony. For a while he surveys the scene of death in stern silence, but soon the memory of his wrongs weighs upon his soul and rouses him to action. He springs upon his feet, and his shrill war-whoop rings through the forest, like the echo of the tap of the woodpecker on the hollow beech. His eye flashes fire as he grasps his war spear, and his laugh, when he examines his good ash bow, is like the cry of a hungry panther. Is not vengeance his? Look at yonder flames! He hath kindled them. Listen to that wail of many over the slaughtered corpses of their friends, who lay down to rest at the beginning of darkness, and woke ere the sun came over the hills in the shades of the valley of death. Bitterly, deeply, deadly, has the son of Alknomook revenged his own, and the wrongs of his race.

Again the dreamer saw, and still his dream was of the land where he dwelt. He saw the two sister Genii sitting in the same spot where he had at first beheld them. She who was of the far clime still retained the beauty and grace which were her's when her little foot first touched the greensward of the hitherto, by her, untrodden island. Still around her head was bound the grape-vine laden with rich, ripe, clusters, amongst which were intermingled locks of hair, of a hue resembling the yellow leaf. Still were her round and plump arms bound with the shining bracelets, and her long and slender fingers adorned with the glittering rings. The sheaf of nodding grain was still an emblem of her power, and the shell and sceptre another. But she wore no more the suppliant air which at first distinguished her. Pride and haughtiness, and command and oppression, were now written on her face, and ruled her gestures.

By her side stood the other Genius, the spirit of the land, her elder sister—but oh, how changed! Her once glossy black locks now hung uncombed upon a shoulder once beautifully rounded, but rounded no longer; her mocassins were torn and soiled; and missing from her wrists and ancles the gay ornaments of bead and shell-work which adorned them in the day of her prosperity and pride. The feathers of the canieu or war-eagle, and the painted vulture, towered above her head no more, and gone from her shoulder was the emblem of the race over which she had borne rule, the bow and the arrow.

Anon these two sisters entered into speech with each other. She who was of the land, from the moment that the Bird of Ages planted it in the bosom of the waters, said to the other,

"Thou hast a most beautiful land."

"It is indeed a most beautiful land," answered the other, casting her eye proudly over the space beneath her feet.

"It has lofty mountains."

"Its mountains are very lofty."

"It has many rapid and beautiful rivers."

"It has."

"Its suns—"

"Are bright as the eyes of a dove in the moon of buds."

"Its winds—"

"Soft and balm-scented as the breath of a young maiden."

"I should like to live in thy cabin, to range uncontrolled through thy green glades, and to listen in dreaming repose to the music of thy merry waterfalls."

"Ah, no doubt thou wouldst, but dost thou think I would permit thee?" replied she, who was once a stranger in the land, but was a stranger no longer.

"Knowest thou not that we are sisters?" asked the dark Genius timidly.

"Nay, I knew it not," replied the other.

"We are, and so thou didst say when thou camest in the white cloud, and I gave thee hills, and mountains, and rivers, and lakes, and glades, and a part of the sea."

"The more fool thou, for admitting one to wrest from thee thy fair possessions."

"I deemed thee in want, and then wert thou not my sister?"

"If thou wert I have forgotten it," replied the other haughtily. "If thou didst me favours, thine impertinence in remembering them hath more than cancelled the obligation. Depart from me, and let me behold thy face no more."

The dark Genius withdrew at the bidding of her haughty sister, and the chief of the Abnakis awoke, and related his dream to his tribe. Hath it not come to pass? Look abroad on the land, and make answer. The race of the red man hath disappeared from the earth, as the snows disappear before the beams of a spring sun, or the hues of purple and gold on the western sky, at the approach of darkness. It is only in the regions of the Hunter's Star, where the pale face dare not venture, that the red man may now be found.

NOTES.

(1) *Foretell the coming of tempests and storms.* — p. 308.

The Indian jugglers — I am not now speaking of those who pretend to cure disease — are sometimes successful in their legerdemain, to a degree, which almost makes a convert of the sceptic. The following story is related by the interesting Carver.

"One day, whilst we were all expressing our wishes for this desirable event, (the arrival of the traders with provisions) and looking from an eminence in hopes of seeing them come over the lake, the chief priest, belonging to the band of the Killistinoes, told us, that he would endeavour to obtain a conference with the Great Spirit, and know from him when the traders would arrive. I paid little attention to this declaration, supposing that it would be productive of some juggling trick, just sufficiently covered to deceive the ignorant Indians. But the king of that tribe telling me that this was chiefly undertaken by the priests, to alleviate my anxiety, and, at the same time, to convince me how much interest he had with the Great Spirit, I thought it necessary to restrain my animadversions on his design.

"The following evening was fixed upon for this spiritual conference. When every thing had been properly prepared, the king came to me and led me to a capacious tent, the covering of which was drawn up, so as to render what was transacting within visible to those who stood without. We found the tent surrounded by a great number of the Indians, but we readily gained admission, and seated ourselves on skins laid on the ground for that purpose. In the centre, I observed that there was a place of an oblong shape, which was composed of stakes stuck in the ground, with intervals between, so as to form a kind of chest or coffin, large enough to contain the body of a man. These were of a middle size, and placed at such a distance from each other, that whatever lay within them was readily to be discerned. The tent was perfectly illuminated by a great number of torches, made of splinters cut from the pine or birch tree, which the Indians held in their hands.

"In a few minutes the priest entered; when an amazing large elk's-skin being spread on the ground, just at my feet, he laid himself down upon it, after having stripped himself of every garment, except that which he wore close about his middle. Being now prostrate on his back, he first laid hold of one side of the skin, and folded it over him, and then the other, leaving only his head uncovered. This was no sooner done, than two of the young men who stood by took about forty yards of strong cord, made also of an elk's hide, and rolled it tight round his body, so that he was completely swathed within the skins. Being thus bound up like an Egyptain Mummy, one took him by the heels and the other by the head, and lifted him over the pales into the enclosure. I could also now discern him as plain as I had hitherto done, and I took care not to turn my eyes a moment from the object before me, that I might the more readily detect the artifice; for such, I doubted not, but that it would turn out to be.

"The priest had not lain in this situation more than a few seconds, when he began to mutter. This he continued to do for some time, and then by degrees grew louder and louder, till at length he spoke articulately; however, what he uttered was in such a mixed jargon of the Chippewas, Ottawas, and Killistinoe languages, that I could understand but very little of it. Having continued in this tone for a considerable while, he at last exerted his voice to its utmost pitch, sometimes raving and sometimes praying, till he had worked himself into such an agitation, that he foamed at his mouth.

"After having remained nearly three quarters of an hour in the place, and continued his vociferation with unabated vigour, he seemed to be quite exhausted, and remained speechless. But in an instant he sprang upon his feet, notwithstanding, at the time he was put in, it appeared impossible for him to move either his legs or arms; and, shaking off his covering as quick as if the bands with which it had been bound were burned asunder, he began to address those who stood around, in a firm and audible voice. 'My brothers,' said he, 'the Great Spirit has deigned to hold a talk with his servant, at my earnest request. He has not, indeed, told me when the persons we expect will be here; but to-morrow, soon after the sun has reached his highest point in the heavens, a canoe will arrive, and the people in that will inform us when the traders will come.'

"Having said this, he stepped out of the enclosure, and, after he had put on his robes, dismissed the assembly.

"I own I was greatly astonished at what I had seen; but as I observed that every eye in the company was fixed on me with a view to discover my sentiments, I carefully concealed every emotion.

"The nest day the sun shone bright, and long before noon all the Indians were gathered together on the eminence that overlooked the lake. The old king came to me and asked me whether I had so much confidence in what the priest had foretold, as to join his people on the hill, and wait for the completion of it? I told him I was at a loss what opinion to form of the prediction, but that I would readily attend him. On this we walked together to the place where the others were assembled. Every eye was again fixed by turns on me and on the lake; when, just as the sun had reached his zenith, agreeable to what the priest had foretold, a canoe came round a point of land about a league distant. The Indians no sooner beheld it, than they set up a universal shout, and by their looks seemed to triumph in the interest their priest thus evidently had with the Great Spirit."

It is related by a Madame de Marson, that she was one day very uneasy about her husband, who commanded at that time a post in Acadia; he was still absent, though the time be had fixed for his return was already past. An Indian woman, seeing Madame de Marson uneasy, asked her the reason of it, and, having learned it, told her, after musing some time on it, not to vex herself, that her husband would return such a day at such an hour, naming both, with a grey hat on his head. As she perceived the lady gave no credit to her prediction, she returned to her at the day and hour she had assigned, and asked her whether she would not come to see her husband arrive, and pressed her so strongly to follow her, that at last she led her to the bank of the river. They had scarcely arrived there, when Mons. de Marson appeared in a canoe, with a grey hat on his head, and being told what had passed, assured them that he was utterly at a loss to conceive which way the Indian woman could know the day and hour of his arrival.

Another well attested story of successful jugglery is related in a History of Virginia, the second edition of which appeared in 1722.

"Some years ago," says the author, "there happened a very dry time, towards the heads of the rivers, and especially on the upper parts of James River, where Colonel Byrd had several quarters of negroes. This gentleman has been for a long time extremely respected and feared by all the Indians round about, who, without knowing the name of any governor, have ever been kept in order by him. During this drought, an Indian, well known to one of the Colonel's overseers, came to him, and asked if his tobacco was not like to be spoiled. The overseer answered, yes, if they had not rain very suddenly. The Indian, who pretended great kindness for his master, told the overseer, if he would promise to give him two bottles of rum, he would bring him rain enough. The overseer did not believe anything of the matter, not seeing at that time the least appearance of rain, nor so much as a cloud in the sky; however, he promised to give him the rum when his master came thither, if he would be as good as his word; upon this the Indian went immediately a *pauwawing*, as they call it; and in about half an hour there came up a black cloud into the sky, that showered down rain enough upon this gentleman's corn and tobacco, but none at all upon any of the neighbours, except a few drops of the skirts of the shower."

With a belief that these tales of Indian *diablerie* will not be uninteresting to the reader, I will relate one more. It is copied from Long's Expedition to the Source of St. Peter's River. "About twenty years ago, a large party of Indians, collected near Lake Travers, were quite destitute of tobacco; not knowing how to procure any, they applied to Tatankanaje (Standing Buffalo), a prophet of some distinction, and the uncle of the present chief of the Kahras. This man usually carried about him a little stone idol, carved into a human shape; this he called his little man, and to it he always applied when consulted in the way of his profession. Tatankanaje, being requested to advise the best means of obtaining tobacco, made answer to them, that if they would go to a certain place which he pointed out to them, they would find his idol, and, by examining it, they would observe in its hand a piece of tobacco. They did as he bade them, and found in the little fellow's hand a piece about four inches long; this was brought to the camp, and was thought to redound much to the credit both of the prophet and the idol; but Tatankanaje then observed that he would consult the little man, and ascertain where he had found the tobacco, and how he came by it. This he did by putting interrogatories to him, to which he pretended that audible answers were returned, though of the many present not one heard them beside himself. The purport of these answers, however, as he subsequently informed them, was, that at a spot on the St. Peter, near to Redwood River, there was a boat loaded with goods; that her commander, a French trader, having been murdered by the Sioux, the crew had been alarmed, and had run away, leaving the boat unguarded, together with her cargo, consisting principally of tobacco; that the little man had seen her, and finding a piece of tobacco on a keg, had brought it up. The prophet having invited them to seek for it, they repaired to the spot, found the boat, took the tobacco, and returned the rest of the goods to the first French traders that passed up the river. This event happened, as we were informed, in the presence of Renville and Freniers, two French traders of reputation, both considered as intelligent and enlightened men; they were the fathers of the two half-breed traders, with whom we were acquainted. The story is given with all the particulars that might be wished for; the name of the owner of the boat was Benjamin La Goterie, a name well known in that country. The story has been current ever since. The traders, who appear to credit it, state that it was impossible for the prophet to have visited the spot and returned without his absence being known, as the distance exceeds one hundred miles; from whom he received his intelligence they never knew. As to the Dahcotahs themselves, they never considered it possible that it might be a knavery of the prophet's, but attributed it altogether to his mystic lore.

"On another occasion, Tatankanaje acquired great reputation in consequence of a prediction that he would lead a war party; that, on the day which he appointed, and at a particular spot which he described, he would fall in with a camp of fifteen Assiniboin lodges; that he would attack and defeat them, kill a certain number of the enemy, and make a stated amount of prisoners: he predicted, in like manner, the loss of lives which would attend this victory. The event justified, as it is said, the prediction; not only as to the general results, but even as to the circumstances of time, place, number of killed and wounded on both sides, and amount of prisoners taken from the enemy. Of course, so valuable a prophet was constantly resorted to for the recovery of stolen property, or of goods that were lost, for a knowledge of the fate of persons that were travelling, for the cure of diseases, and for all such other important points, upon which the credulity both of civilized and savage man induces them to lend a willing ear to the impositions of knaves. Of his talent in recovering property, we regret that we can only mention a circumstance in which the object at stake was very trifling. Some one had ventured to steal away the prophet's bridle; it was concealed in a lodge that formed one in a camp of one hundred lodges. The prophet took a mirror in his hand, and walked round the village, until, as he said, he saw the lost bridle reflected in his mirror: he entered the adjoining lodge, and recovered his property.

"Not only do they prophesy, but they perform tricks of legerdemain, all which they ascribe to the success of their incantations. We are indebted to Mr. Charles Hess, a French trader, with whom Mr. Say had several conferences at Fort St. Anthony, for the account of a trick performed by an Assiniboin. The magician asserted, in Mr. Hess's presence, as well as in that of many Indians, that he could cause water to flow into an empty keg, though he might at that time be upon a dry prairie, and at a distance from any spring or stream. Mr. Hess having told him that he did not believe him, but that, if he succeeded, he would give him a keg of whiskey, the Indian offered to repeat the trick. He exhibited to them his keg, which they examined, and all judged to be empty. The bung was removed, the cask turned over, and no liquid issued from it. The Indian then commenced his incantations, raising his keg towards the heavens, dancing and performing many unmeaning gestures; after which he presented it to the Indian chief that was present, bidding him to drink of the water which it contained; the latter drank of it, found it very good, and passed it to his neighbour; the cask was circulated, to the great satisfaction of all the Indians, who drank of its contents, and even Mr. Hess was convinced that the keg really held pure water."

(2) *Tattooed Warrior.* — p. 316.

This expression may be hardly used of the tribes to which the tale relates. Tattooing, in the sense in which it is commonly spoken of, was never, as far as I have learnt, in use among the Indians, occupying the tract of country which is now called New England.

Among those tribes with whom the practice is in use, the process of tattooing is performed by persons who make it a business of profit. Their instrument consists of three or four needles, tied to a truncated and flattened end of a stick, in such an arrangement, that the points may form a straight line; the figure desired is traced upon the skin, and some dissolved gunpowder, or pulverised charcoal, is pricked in with the instrument, agreeably to the figure. It is said not to be painful, but it is sometimes accompanied by inflammation and fever, and has been known to terminate fatally.

(3) *Disgraced Woman.* — p. 319.

Not to have borne children is one of the deepest and most indelible disgraces that can be endured by an Indian wife. She becomes a standing theme of ridicule to those of her own sex who are blest with children. The pride and honour of parents among them depend upon the number of their family. Another reason why barrenness is disgraceful, is, that it is considered to be brought on by incontinence or wilful abortions.

END OF THE SECOND VOLUME.

FOOTNOTES:

[1] Little Wise People, the Beavers, so called by the Assiniboins. The Indians, though they kill this animal whenever they can, nevertheless esteem him scarcely inferior to man in wisdom. A bit of his skin, or his paw, or any part of him, is esteemed a very powerful "medicine" or amulet.

[2] See this superstition in the last tale.

[3] The Indians always give a corporeal form to the Supreme Being, and, in every instance that I have heard of, when supposing him to have a human form, imagine him with some kind of covering upon his head. Since their introduction to the white people, they have invariably supposed this covering to be a hat.

[4] Chesapeak Bay.

[5] See the Tradition *post*.

[6] The greater part of the Indians of the Western Continent believe themselves descended from, or colonies of, the Lenni Lenapes, and hence give to that tribe the epithet, "grandfather." Several of the tribes have a tradition, that they came from beyond the Rocky Mountains.

[7] Oniagarah, Niagara: the former is the Indian pronunciation of the name of that celebrated cataract.

[8] See the note relating to the Mammoth in the tradition of "The Coming of Miquon."

[9] Intoxicating bean.—See Long's First Expedition to the Rocky Mountains.

[10] See the tradition, entitled "The Valley of the Bright Old Inhabitants."

[11] When an Indian wishes to express his admiration of music, he likens it to the notes of the Mocking-Bird. When the Winnabagoes visited Philadelphia, in the winter of 1828, they went to the Chesnut-street theatre, to hear Mrs. Knight sing: one of the chiefs, wishing to testify his delight, plucked an eagle's feather, and sent it

to her by the box-keeper, with the message, that "she was a mocking-bird squaw." — *American paper.*

[12] The *physic-nut*, or Indian olive. The Indians, when they go in pursuit of deer, carry this fruit with them, supposing that it has the power of charming or drawing that creature to them.

[13] Button snakeroot.

[14] Tobacco.

[15] The Spaniards.

[16] The partridge, a common figure with the Indians to express cowardice.

[17] Northern lights, *aurora borealis.*

[18] The milky way.

[19] The name given by the Indians to the bellows.

[20] Put the hatchet under the bedstead, an Indian figure, signifying that peace will not last long.

[21] A night's encampment is a halt of one year at a place.

[22] The Shoshonees, a tribe living west of the Rocky Mountains, to indicate the sincerity of their professions, pull off their mocassins before they smoke in the pipe of peace, an action which imprecates on themselves the misery of going barefoot for ever, if they are faithless to their words.

[23] "Great council fire" means all the land or territory possessed by the nation.

[24] Michabou is generally the Indian Neptune: sometimes, however, they mean by this title the Great Spirit.

[25] The mountains.

[26] Hills of the Serpent, the Rocky Mountains. I have before mentioned the Indian superstition that thunder is the hissing of a great serpent, which has his residence among those mountains.

[27] Hollow voice — echo.

[28] Martha's Vineyard, a little island upon the coast of New England.

[29] The owl. See the tradition, vol. 1. p. 61.

[30] A brook in Barnstable County, respecting which this tradition is current among the Indians.

[31] The Indians, as I have before remarked, believe the world to be an island, and always speak of it as such.

[32] Gayhead, which has a chalk cliff.

[33] See note, vol. i. page 59.

[34] See note, vol. i. page 253.

[35] "Wrathful phial of liquid fire" is a literal translation of the Chippewa word for ardent spirit.

[36] Burning water, ardent spirits, commonly called by them the "fire-eater."